About This Book

Why is this topic important?

Learning to solve problems is perhaps the most important skill that students can acquire. In professional contexts, people are paid to solve problems, not complete exams, and in everyday life, we constantly solve problems. In *All Life Is Problem Solving*, Karl Popper argues that we face problems, big and small, simple and complex, clear and confusing every day in our lives. However, educators have largely ignored teaching how to learn to solve problems. This book is about problem solving and seeks to address this issue.

What can you achieve with this book?

The purpose of this book is to illustrate how problems vary and how different teaching methods can be used to match these various types of problems. The book is intended to raise your awareness about the importance and the complexities of helping people to learn to solve problems. By applying the instructional design methods described in this book to problems in your own curriculum, you can help your learners become better problem solvers.

How is this book organized?

The book has eight chapters. Chapter One makes the case for treating problems differently by describing different kinds of problems and how they vary. Chapter Two identifies the components of learning environments to support learning how to solve story problems, troubleshooting problems, and case and system analysis problems. Chapter Three examines different approaches to representing problems to learners, including problem posing, anchoring problems in macrocontexts, and case-based instruction. Chapter Four describes technology-based tools for helping learners mentally represent problems for themselves, including semantic networks, causal modeling, influence diagrams, expert systems, and dynamic systems models. Chapter Five addresses methods for associating different solutions to problems, including worked examples, case libraries, and cognitive flexibility hypertexts. Chapter Six looks at methods for generating and testing hypotheses, including simulations and argumentation. Chapter Seven discusses processes for reflecting on the problem-solving process: peer instruction, thinking-aloud pair problem solving, teachbacks, abstracted replays, and coding verbal protocols. Finally, Chapter Eight tackles perhaps the most vexing issue: how to assess problem solving. This final chapter offers three approaches to assessing problem solving: performance assessment, component skills, and argumentation.

About Pfeiffer

Pfeiffer serves the professional development and hands-on resource needs of training and human resource practitioners and gives them products to do their jobs better. We deliver proven ideas and solutions from experts in HR development and HR management, and we offer effective and customizable tools to improve workplace performance. From novice to seasoned professional, Pfeiffer is the source you can trust to make yourself and your organization more successful.

Essential Knowledge Pfeiffer produces insightful, practical, and comprehensive materials on topics that matter the most to training and HR professionals. Our Essential Knowledge resources translate the expertise of seasoned professionals into practical, how-to guidance on critical workplace issues and problems. These resources are supported by case studies, worksheets, and job aids and are frequently supplemented with CD-ROMs, websites, and other means of making the content easier to read, understand, and use.

Essential Tools Pfeiffer's Essential Tools resources save time and expense by offering proven, ready-to-use materials—including exercises, activities, games, instruments, and assessments—for use during a training or team-learning event. These resources are frequently offered in looseleaf or CD-ROM format to facilitate copying and customization of the material.

Pfeiffer also recognizes the remarkable power of new technologies in expanding the reach and effectiveness of training. While e-hype has often created whizbang solutions in search of a problem, we are dedicated to bringing convenience and enhancements to proven training solutions. All our e-tools comply with rigorous functionality standards. The most appropriate technology wrapped around essential content yields the perfect solution for today's on-the-go trainers and human resource professionals.

www.pfeiffer.com

Essential resources for training and HR professionals

ABOUT THE INSTRUCTIONAL TECHNOLOGY AND TRAINING SERIES

INSTRUCTIONAL TECHNOLOGY & TRAINING SERIES

This comprehensive series responds to the rapidly changing training field by focusing on all forms of instructional and training technology—from the well-known to the emerging and state-of-the-art approaches. These books take a broad view of technology, which is viewed as systematized, practical knowledge that improves productivity. For many, such knowledge is typically equated with computer applications; however, we see it as also encompassing other nonmechanical strategies such as systematic design processes or new tactics for working with individuals and groups of learners.

The series is also based upon a recognition that the people working in the training community are a diverse group. They have a wide range of professional experience, expertise, and interests. Consequently, this series is dedicated to two distinct goals: helping those new to technology and training become familiar with basic principles and techniques, and helping those seasoned in the training field become familiar with cutting-edge practices. The books for both groups are rooted in solid research, but are still designed to help readers readily apply what they learn.

The Instructional Technology and Training Series is directed to persons working in many roles, including trainers and training managers, business leaders, instructional designers, instructional facilitators, and consultants. These books are also geared for practitioners who want to know how to apply technology to training and learning in practical, results-driven ways. Experts and leaders in the field who need to explore the more advanced, high-level practices that respond to the growing pressures and complexities of today's training environment will find indispensable tools and techniques in this groundbreaking series of books.

Rita C. Richey
William J. Rothwell
Timothy W. Spannaus
Series Editors

Kent L. Gustafson
M. David Merrill
Allison Rossett
Advisory Board

Learning to Solve Problems

An Instructional Design Guide

DAVID H. JONASSEN

Pfeiffer

A Wiley Imprint
www.pfeiffer.com

Copyright © 2004 by John Wiley & Sons, Inc.

Published by Pfeiffer
An Imprint of Wiley
989 Market Street, San Francisco, CA 94103-1741   www.pfeiffer.com

For additional copies/bulk purchases of this book in the U.S. please contact 800-274-4434.

Pfeiffer books and products are available through most bookstores. To contact Pfeiffer directly call our Customer Care Department within the U.S. at 800-274-4434, outside the U.S. at 317-572-3985, fax 317-572-4002, or on-line at www.pfeiffer.com.

Pfeiffer also publishes its books in a variety of electronic formats. Some content that appears in print may not be available in electronic books.

ISBN: 0-7879-6437-9

Library of Congress Cataloging-in-Publication Data

Jonassen, David H., date.
   Learning to solve problems : an instructional design guide / David H.
   Jonassen.
     p. cm.
   Includes bibliographical references and index.
   ISBN 0-7879-6437-9 (alk. paper)
   1. Instructional systems—Design. 2. Problem solving—Study and
teaching. I. Title.
   LB1028.38.J645   2003
   371.39—dc22
                                          2003018771

Acquiring Editor: Matthew Davis   Manufacturing Supervisor: Bill Matherly
Director of Development: Kathleen Dolan Davies   Editorial Assistant: Laura Reizman
Production Editor: Nina Kreiden   Illustrations: Lotus Art
Editor: Beverly Miller

Printed in the United States of America

Printing   10 9 8 7 6 5 4 3 2 1

To **ROSE**, who provides more solutions than problems

CONTENTS

LIST OF FIGURES, TABLES, AND EXHIBITS

Figures

Table

Exhibits

ACKNOWLEDGMENTS

I WANT to thank Rob Foshay, who provided the impetus for this journey into problem solving.

We cannot forget Herb Simon, who introduced the field of psychology to the problems of problem solving.

I wish to acknowledge many of my students, who have forced me to expand and clarify my ideas.

L EARNING TO SOLVE problems is the most important skill that
students can learn in any setting. In professional contexts, people are paid
to solve problems, not to complete exams. In everyday life, we constantly solve
problems. Karl Popper stated this maxim most clearly in his book *All Life Is
Problem Solving* (1999). We face problems, big and small, simple and complex, clear and confusing every day in our lives. But as a field, educators have
largely ignored how to learn to solve problems.

There is virtually no instructional design literature on problem solving.
Bob Gagné referred to problem solving in his early editions of the *Conditions
of Learning,* but in later editions, he gave up on it, preferring instead to deal
with higher-order rules (similar to story problems). Why is that? If problems
are pandemic and so essential to everyday and professional activity, why do
we not exert more effort in helping students learn to solve problems?

Over the past three decades, a number of information-processing models
of problem solving, such as the classic General Problem Solver (Newell and

Simon, 1972), have sought to explain problem solving. The General Problem Solver specifies two sets of thinking processes associated with problem-solving processes: understanding processes and search processes. Another popular problem-solving model, the IDEAL problem solver (Bransford and Stein, 1993), describes problem solving as a uniform process of *I*dentifying potential problems, *D*efining and representing the problem, *E*xploring possible strategies, *A*cting on those strategies, and *L*ooking back and evaluating the effects of those activities. Although the IDEAL model assumes that these processes are applied differently to different problems, no explicit suggestions are made for how to do this. Gick (1986) synthesized these and other problem-solving models (Greeno, 1978) into a simplified model of the problem-solving process: the processes of constructing a problem representation, searching for solutions, and implementing and monitoring solutions. Although these problem-solving models are descriptively useful, they tend to treat all problems the same in an effort to articulate a generalizable problem-solving procedure. The culmination of information-processing concepts was an attempt, albeit unsuccessful, to articulate a uniform theory of problem solving (Smith, 1991).

The underlying assumption of this book, as I note in Chapter One, is that problem solving is a special kind of learning outcome quite unlike other learning outcomes. Moreover, there are many different kinds of problem solving, and each requires different forms of teaching and learning support. For example, solving a math problem calls on a different set of content knowledge and skills from solving an international political dilemma. This book addresses both problems by describing different kinds of problem solving and models for designing interactive learning environments to support how to learn to solve different kinds of problems.

Problem-Based Learning

This book is not about problem-based learning (PBL), which may be the most significant pedagogical innovation in the history of education. PBL, as it has been implemented in medical schools around the world, is a systemic approach to preparing medical doctors to be problem solvers, because that is the nature of their job. PBL redefines curriculum and pedagogy in terms of problem-solving activities. It improves not only problem-solving abilities but retention as well (Koslowski, Okagaki, Lorenz, and Umbach, 1989).

There are at least two problems with PBL as a movement. First, there is no agreement on what PBL means. Although the medical model of PBL is fairly well circumscribed, *PBL* is a term that is used pandemically to represent just about anything—from solving textbook problems to serving apprenticeships. The second problem with PBL is that it is a pedagogical innovation that employs only one model for supporting problem solving. In this book, I argue that learning to solve different kinds of problems requires different kinds of instructional support.

Overview of the Book

In Chapter One, I make the case for treating problems differently by describing different kinds of problems and how they vary.

Beginning in Chapter Two and continuing throughout most of the rest of the book, I describe how to design instruction to support three kinds of problems: story problems; troubleshooting; and case, system, or policy analysis problems. These are not the only kinds of problems there are. (See Jonassen, 2000a, for a more complete typology of problems.) They do, however, represent the range of different kinds of problems. After this book, my focus turns to better understanding design problems, which are perhaps the most important, albeit complex, kind of problem to learn to solve. Although case analysis problems share attributes with design problems, design problems are special and deserve special treatment. In Chapter Two, I describe the components of learning environments to support learning how to solve story problems, troubleshooting problems, and case and system analysis problems.

In Chapters Three through Six, I describe in greater depth different methods for supporting each of these kinds of problem solving. Chapter Three looks at approaches to representing problems to learners, including problem posing, anchoring problems in macrocontexts, and case-based instruction.

Chapter Four explores technology-based tools for helping learners to mentally represent problems for themselves, including semantic networks, causal modeling, influence diagrams, expert systems, and dynamic systems. Adequately representing problems is the key to problem solving, I believe. Chapter Five describes methods for associating different solutions to problems, including worked examples, case libraries, and cognitive flexibility hypertexts. Chapter Six examines methods for generating and testing hypotheses, including simulations and argumentation.

At the beginning of each chapter, I make general suggestions about which kinds of problems can be supported by each of these activities. Although there exists some empirical support for using these methods to support learning to solve problems, we need research to clarify the roles of these methods. That will be the focus of my research for years to come, and I hope that others will also support the research on problem solving.

Chapter Seven more generally discusses different processes for reflecting on the problem-solving process, including peer instruction, think-aloud pair problem solving, teachbacks, abstracted replays, and coding verbal protocols. Learning and problem solving are active processes. Learning from activity requires reflection on that activity.

Finally, Chapter Eight tackles perhaps the most vexing of problems related to problem solving: how to assess it. In order to adequately assess a skill as complex as problem solving, more than one kind of assessment is required. I suggest three—performance assessment, component skills, and argumentation—and illustrate ways to use them to assess problem solving,

My primary goal for this book is to raise the awareness of educators about the importance and the complexities of helping people learn to solve problems. A bit of reflection on your own experience will reveal how common problems are and how important learning to solve them is. There is much work that remains to be done in this area. This book is meant to foster interest in that enterprise.

Learning to
Solve Problems

1

What Is Problem Solving?

LEARNING IN THE everyday world, where people live and work, is omnipresent and essential to survival, let alone progress. In homes, businesses, organizations, and societies in every culture, learning is driven by problems that need solving. How do I pay for a new car? Which schools should my children attend? How do we design a new marketing campaign to address a target market? How do we make peace with our enemies? What's wrong with the compressor? How do we raise funds to support municipal services?

Modern life in nearly every context presents a deluge of problems that demand solutions. Although many trainers avoid using the word *problem* because it implies acquiescence and insolubility (a problem with problem solving is that *problem* has many meanings), intellectually that is what they get paid to do. Designing training is an archetype of design problem solving. And most of these problems that people face in their everyday lives are ill structured. They are not the well-structured problems that students at every level of schooling, from kindergarten through graduate school, attempt to solve at the back of every textbook chapter.

The ubiquity of problems in our lives and the limited amount of time that always seems to be allocated to education and learning lead me to argue two things. First, telling students what we know about the world and quizzing their recall of what we told them is not only an insult to our learners (we should expect more of them); that pedagogy also retards their epistemological development, preventing them from developing the knowledge-seeking skills they need (Jonassen, Marra, and Palmer, 2004).

The second point that I argue is that the only legitimate goal of education and training should be problem solving. Why? Because people need to learn how to solve problems in order to function in their everyday and professional lives. No one in the everyday world gets paid for memorizing facts and taking exams. Most people get paid for solving problems. Content, the coin of the educational realm, is relatively meaningless outside the context of a problem. From kindergarten through graduate school, students study content without clear purpose or reason. If they studied content for the explicit purpose of solving problems, the content would have more meaning. Second, what is learned in the context of solving problems is better comprehended and better retained. Some educators, however, believe that if education is focused on solving problems, students will miss the breadth of learning that is reflected in the curriculum. That is probably true, but they will learn more.

Let us compare a couple of learning equations. Students who memorize information for the test usually retain less than 10 percent of what they learn, so 10 percent of the whole curriculum (100 percent assuming that the teacher or trainer can cover the whole curriculum) yields a 10 percent learning outcome (and it is probably less than that). In a problem-oriented curriculum, students may cover only 50 percent of the curriculum, but they understand and remember 50 percent of what they learn, yielding a 25 percent learning outcome. These figures cannot be validated in different contexts, but the point is simple: when students are solving problems, they learn and comprehend more. Remember the most important lessons that you have learned in your life. They probably resulted from solving some kind of problem.

What Are Problems, and How Do They Vary?

Just what is a problem? There are at least two critical attributes in my definition of a problem. First, a problem is an unknown entity in some context (the difference between a goal state and a current state). Second, finding or solving for the unknown must have some social, cultural, or intellectual value. That is, someone believes that it is worth finding the unknown. If no one perceives an unknown or a need to determine an unknown, there is no perceived problem.

There are a number of variable attributes of problems. Problems vary in knowledge needed to solve them, the form they appear in, and the processes needed to solve them. The problems themselves also vary considerably, from simple addition problems in elementary school to complex social-cultural-political problems like those encountered in the Middle East. Intellectually, problems vary in at least four ways: structuredness, complexity, dynamicity, and domain specificity or abstractness.

Structuredness

Problems within domains and between domains vary in terms of how well structured they are. Jonassen (1997) described problems on a continuum from well structured to ill structured. The most common problems that students solve in schools, universities, and training venues are well-structured problems. Like the story problems found at the end of textbook chapters or on examinations, well-structured problems require the application of a limited and known number of concepts, rules, and principles being studied within a restricted domain. They have a well-defined initial state, a known goal state or solution, and a constrained set of logical operators (a known procedure for solving). Well-structured problems also present all elements of the problem to the learners, and they have knowable, comprehensible solutions.

Ill-structured problems, at the other end of the continuum, are the kinds of problems that are more often encountered in everyday and professional practice. Also known as wicked problems, these problems do not necessarily conform to the content domains being studied, so their solutions are neither predictable nor convergent. Ill-structured problems are also interdisciplinary, that is, they cannot be solved by applying concepts and principles from a single domain. For example, solutions to problems such as local pollution may require the application of concepts and principles from math, science, political science, sociology, economics, and psychology. Ill-structured problems often possess aspects that are unknown (Wood, 1983), and they possess multiple solutions or solution methods or often no solutions at all (Kitchner, 1983). Frequently, multiple criteria are required for evaluating solutions to ill-structured problems, and sometimes the criteria are not known at all. Ill-structured problems often require learners to make judgments and express personal opinions or beliefs about the problem.

For a long time, psychologists believed that "in general, the processes used to solve ill-structured problems are the same as those used to solve well structured problems" (Simon, 1978, p. 287). However, more recent research in everyday problem solving in different contexts makes clear distinctions between thinking required to solve well-structured problems and everyday problems. Dunkle, Schraw, and Bendixen (1995) concluded that performance in solving well-defined problems is independent of performance on ill-defined tasks, with ill-defined problems engaging a different set of epistemic beliefs. Hong, Jonassen, and McGee (2003) showed that solving ill-structured problems in a simulation called on different skills than well-structured problems did, including the use of metacognition and argumentation (see Chapter Six). Other studies have shown differences in required processing for well-structured and ill-structured problems. For example, communication patterns among problem solvers differed while teams solved well-structured versus ill-structured problems (Jonassen and Kwon, 2001). Groups that solved ill-structured problems produced more extensive arguments in support of their solutions when solving ill-structured problems because of the importance of generating and supporting alternative solutions (Cho and Jonassen, 2002).

Although the need for more research comparing well-structured and ill-structured problems is obvious, it seems reasonable to predict that different intellectual skills are required to solve well-structured than ill-structured problems, and therefore the ways that we teach people to solve well-structured problems cannot be used effectively to teach people to solve ill-structured problems. Probably some very ill-structured problems cannot be taught at all. They must be experienced and dealt with using general intelligence and world knowledge.

Complexity

Problems vary in terms of their complexity. Problem complexity is determined by the number of issues, functions, or variables involved in the problem; the degree of connectivity among those variables; the type of functional relationships among those properties; and the stability among the properties of the problem over time (Funke, 1991). Simple problems, like textbook problems, are composed of few variables, while ill-structured problems may include many factors or variables that may interact in unpredictable ways. For example, international political problems are complex and unpredictable. Complexity is also concerned with how many, how clearly, and how reliably components are represented in the problem. We know that problem difficulty is related to problem complexity (English, 1998). The idea of problem complexity seems to be intuitively recognizable by even untrained learners (Suedfield, de Vries, Bluck, and Wallbaum, 1996). The primary reason is that complex problems involve more cognitive operations than simpler ones do (Kluwe, 1995). Balancing multiple variables during problem structuring and solution generation places a heavy cognitive burden on problem solvers.

Complexity and structuredness overlap. Ill-structured problems tend to be more complex, especially those emerging from everyday practice. Most well-structured problems tend to be less complex; however, some well-structured problems can be extremely complex and ill-structured problems can be fairly simple. For example, video games can be very complex well-structured problems, while selecting what to wear from our closet for different occasions is a simple ill-structured problem (at least for some of us).

Dynamicity

Problems vary in their stability or dynamicity. More complex problems tend to be dynamic; that is, the task environment and its factors change over time. When the conditions of a problem change, the solver must continuously adapt his or her understanding of the problem while searching for new solutions, because the old solutions may no longer be viable. For example, investing in the stock market is often difficult because market conditions (for example, demand, interest rates, or confidence) tend to change, often dramatically, over short periods of time. Static problems are those where the factors are stable over time. Ill-structured problems tend to be more dynamic, and well-structured problems tend to be fairly stable.

Domain (Context) Specificity/Abstractness

Most contemporary research and theory in problem solving claims that problem-solving skills are domain and context specific. That is, problem-solving activities are situated, embedded, and therefore dependent on the nature of the context or domain knowledge. Mathematicians solve problems differently from engineers, who solve problems differently from political scientists, and so on. Problems in one organizational context are solved differently than they are in another context. Problems at IBM are solved differently from those at Hewlett-Packard. They have different organizational structures, different cultures, and different sociological mixes, all of which affect the kinds of problems that arise and how they are solved. Problems within a domain rely on cognitive operations that are specific to that domain (Mayer, 1992; Smith, 1991; Sternberg and Frensch, 1991). For example, students in the probabilistic sciences of psychology and medicine perform better on statistical, methodological, and conditional reasoning problems than do students in law and chemistry, who do not learn such forms of reasoning (Lehman, Lempert, and Nisbett, 1988). The cognitive operations required to solve problems within a domain or context are learned through the development of pragmatic reasoning rather than results from solving that kind of problem. Individuals in different domains or contexts develop reasoning skills through solving ill-structured problems that are situated in those different domains or contexts and require forms of logic that are specific to that domain or context.

In sum, problems within a domain or context vary in terms of their structuredness, complexity, and dynamicity, but all problems vary also along another dimension between domains or contexts. Which affects problems more, context or problem type, is not known.

What Is Problem Solving, and How Does It Vary?

If a problem is an unknown worth solving, then problem solving is "any goal-directed sequence of cognitive operations" (Anderson, 1980, p. 257) directed at finding that unknown. Those operations have two critical attributes. First, problem solving requires the mental representation of the problem and its context. That is, human problem solvers construct a mental representation (or mental model) of the problem, known as the *problem space* (Newell and Simon, 1972). Although there is little agreement on the meaning of mental models or problem spaces, internal mental models (as opposed to social or team mental models) of problems are multimodal representations consisting of structural knowledge, procedural knowledge, reflective knowledge, images and metaphors of the system, and executive or strategic knowledge (Jonassen and Henning, 1999). That is, mental models consist of knowledge about the structure of the problem, knowledge of how to perform tests and other problem-solving activities, the envisionment of the problem and its constituent parts (De Kleer and Brown, 1981), and knowledge of when and how to use procedures. The mental models of experienced problem solvers integrate these different kinds of knowledge, and it is the mental construction of the problem space that is the most critical for problem solving. Second, successful problem solving requires that learners actively manipulate and test their models. Thinking is internalized activity (Jonassen, 2002), especially when solving problems, so knowledge and activity are reciprocal, interdependent processes (Fishbein and others, 1990). We know what we do, and we do what we know. Successful problem solving requires that learners generate and try out solutions in their minds (mental models or problem spaces) before trying them out in the physical world.

If problems differ in terms of structure, complexity, and context, then so too must the kinds of problem-solving processes. How many kinds of problem solving are there? Jonassen (2000a) described a typology of problems, including puzzles, algorithms, story problems, rule-using problems, decision making, troubleshooting, diagnosis-solution problems, strategic performance, systems analysis, design problems, and dilemmas. Table 1–1 describes characteristics of each kind of problem solving. Note that this typology (not taxonomy) described my mental model of problem solving in the year 2000. Additional research and experience may verify more or fewer kinds of problems.

Table 1–1. Kinds of Problems.

Problem Type	Logical Problem	Algorithm	Story Problem	Rule-Using Problem	Decision Making
Learning activity	Logical control and manipulation of limited variables; solve puzzle	Procedural sequence of manipulations; algorithmic process applied to similar sets of variables; calculating or producing correct answer	Disambiguate variables; select and apply algorithm to produce correct answer using prescribed method	Procedural process constrained by rules; select and apply rules to produce system-constrained answers or products	Identifying benefits and limitations; weighting options; selecting alternative and justifying
Inputs	Puzzle	Formula or procedure	Story with formula or procedure embedded	Situation in constrained system; finite rules	Decision situation with limited alternative outcomes
Success criteria	Efficient manipulation; number of moves or manipulations required	Answer or product matches in values and form	Answer or product matches in values and form; correct algorithm used	Productivity (number of relevant or useful answers or products)	Answer or product matches in values and form
Context	Abstract task	Abstract, formulaic	Constrained to predefined elements, shallow context	Purposeful academic, real world, constrained	Life decisions
Structuredness	Discovered	Procedural predictable	Well-defined problem classes; procedural predictable	Unpredicted outcome	Finite outcomes
Abstractness	Abstract, discovery	Abstract, procedural	Limited simulation	Need based	Personally situated

Trouble-shooting	Diagnosis-Solution	Strategic Performance	Case Analysis	Designs	Dilemmas
Examine system; run tests; evaluate results; hypothesize and confirm fault states using strategies (replace, serial elimination, space split)	Troubleshoot system faults; select and evaluate treatment options and monitor; apply problem schemas	Applying tactics to meet strategy in real time; complex performance maintaining situational awareness	Solution identification, alternative actions, argue position	Acting on goals to produce artifact; problem structuring and articulation	Reconciling complex, nonpredictive, vexing decision with no solution; perspectives irreconcilable
Malfunctioning system with one or more faults	Complex system with faults and numerous optional solutions	Real-time, complex performance with competing needs	Complex, leisure-time system with multiple ill-defined goals	Vague goal statement with few constraints; requires structuring	Situation with antinomous positions
Fault(s) identification; efficiency of fault isolation	Strategy used; effectiveness and efficiency of treatment; justification of treatment selected	Achieving strategic objective	Multiple, unclear	Multiple, undefined criteria; no right or wrong, only better or worse	Articulated preference with some justification
Closed system, real world	Real world, technical, mostly closed system	Real-time performance	Real world, constrained	Complex, real-world degrees of freedom; limited input and feedback	Topical, complex, inter-disciplinary
Finite faults and outcomes	Finite faults and outcomes	Ill-structured strategies; well-structured tactics	Ill-structured	Ill-structured	Finite outcomes, multiple reasoning
Problem situated	Problem situated	Contextually situated	Case situated	Problem situated	Issue situated

Source: From Jonassen (2000a).

Regardless of how many kinds of problems there are, I believe that there are similarities in the cognitive processing engaged within these classes of problems. Within classes, there are differences in problem solving depending on the domain or context in which the problem occurs and its structuredness and complexity. Because it is practically impossible to design and develop models, methods, and tools for solving problems in every domain, this book focuses on three different kinds of problems. My goal is to show how methods for representing problems, assessing solutions, and designing learning environments vary across problem types because one of the underlying principles of instructional design is that different learning outcomes engage different learning processes and therefore require different conditions of learning (Gagné, 1960). I want to show how these problem types differ and how instruction to support them should also differ. However, space limitations prevent illustrating models and methods for each of the eleven types of problems identified in the typology in Table 1-1, and, frankly, I have not constructed all of those models yet. So I have chosen three commonly encountered yet divergent kinds of problems to illustrate methods throughout the book: story problems, troubleshooting problems, and case or system or policy analysis problems. I next describe each of these kinds of problems and in Chapter Two describe models for teaching students how to solve each of these three kinds of problems. Chapters Three through Six elucidate the methods described in Chapter Two. Chapter Seven describes a variety of methods to help students reflect on problem-solving processes because reflection is essential to meaningful learning. Finally, Chapter Eight then describes how to assess problem solving for each kind of problem.

Story Problems

From simple problems in beginning mathematics to complex story problems in engineering dynamics classes, story problems are the most commonly used and extensively researched kind of problems. Found at the back of thousands of textbook chapters, these problems are usually, though not most effectively, solved by learners by identifying key words in the story, selecting the appropriate algorithm and sequence for solving the problem, applying the algorithm, and checking their responses, which they hope will be correct (Sherrill,

1983). Story problem solving requires not only calculation accuracy but also the comprehension of textual information, the capacity to visualize the data, the capacity to recognize the semantic structure of the problem, the capacity to sequence their solution activities correctly, and the capacity and willingness to evaluate the procedure that they used to solve the problem (Lucangelli, Tressoldi, and Cendron, 1998).

What do these mean? Different kinds of story problems have different semantic structures, so successfully solving these problems requires that learners develop semantic models of the deep structure of the problem as well as a model of the processing operations required to solve the problem (Riley and Greeno, 1988). Solving story problems requires significant conceptual understanding of the problem class. Based on an extensive analysis of story problem solving, Jonassen (2003) found that solving any kind of story problem requires that learners construct a mental model of the problem type that includes a model of the situation depicted in the surface content, as well as a semantic model of the structure of the problem. For example, simple mathematics motion problems typically use trains, cars, or airplanes traveling in one direction or another as the surface content. In order to be able to solve motion problems, the learner relates trains, cars, and planes to a semantic model of the relationships between the different entities in a problem. For example, there are different kinds of motion problems, such as overtake (one vehicle starts and is followed later by a second, which travels over same route at faster rate), opposite direction (two vehicles leaving the same point are traveling in opposite directions), round trip (a vehicle travels from point A to B and returns), or closure (two vehicles start at different points traveling toward one another) (Mayer, Larkin, and Kadane, 1984). Each kind of motion problem has a different set of structural relations between the problem entities that call on different processing operations. Story problems require that learners understand the situational and structural relationships between the problem entities. Associating situational and structural models leads to comprehension of different classes of story problems. These classes of problems are domain specific. Chemistry problems have different situations and structures than physics problems do, which differ from biology problems.

An analysis of the cognitive requirements for solving story problems shows that learners must do the following things:

- Parse the problem statement, that is, read and break down the description of the problem.
- Try to classify the problem type by:

  Comparing the surface content of the problem to problems previously solved or to problem class descriptions.

  Comparing structural relationships described in the problem to problem models or to previously solved problems.

- Construct a mental representation of the problem being solved by:

  Identifying problem entities (sets) from the surface content.

  Mapping those sets onto the structural model of the problem.

  Accessing the formula and processing operations required to solve the problem.

- Map the values in each set onto the formula.
- Estimate the size of the solution and the proper units (distance, length, and so forth).
- Solve the formula.
- Reconcile the value with the estimate in terms of size and units. (Was the result similar to the estimate?)
- Remember the problem content and the structure of the problem entities and file according to problem type.

In Chapter Two, I will describe a model for designing instruction to support learning to solve story problems.

Troubleshooting Problems

Troubleshooting is among the most commonly experienced kinds of problem solving in the professional world. From troubleshooting a faulty modem to a multiplexed refrigeration system in a modern supermarket, troubleshooting attempts to isolate fault states in some dysfunctional system. Once the fault is found, the part is replaced or repaired.

Troubleshooting is often thought of as a linear series of decisions that leads to fault isolation. That approach may work for helping novices solve simple troubleshooting problems, but it is inadequate for training competent, professional troubleshooters because troubleshooting is not merely a series of decisions. Effective troubleshooting requires system knowledge (conceptual knowledge of how the system works), procedural knowledge (how to perform problem-solving procedures and test activities), and strategic knowledge (knowing when, where, and why to apply procedures) (Pokorny, Hall, Gallaway, and Dibble, 1996). These components comprise the troubleshooter's mental model of the process, which consists of conceptual, functional, and declarative knowledge, including knowledge of system components and interactions, flow control, fault states (fault characteristics, symptoms, contextual information, and probabilities of occurrence), and fault testing procedures. These skills are integrated and organized by the troubleshooter's experiences.

The best predictor of a troubleshooter's skills is the number of similar problems that she or he has solved. Learning to troubleshoot is best facilitated by experience. Technicians through physicians can recall with extraordinary accuracy problems that they have troubleshot many years before. The problems that are most completely and accurately recalled are those that are most difficult to solve, because the problem solver was more conceptually engaged in the process. The primary differences between expert and novice troubleshooters are the amount and organization of system knowledge (Johnson, 1988). An analysis of the cognitive processes required to solve troubleshooting problems shows that learners must:

- Identify the fault state and related symptoms, that is, define the current state of the system being troubleshot.
- Construct a mental model of the problem by:

  Describing the goal state (how do you know when system is functioning properly).

  Identifying the faulty subsystem (known as space splitting).

- Diagnose the problem by:

    Examining the faulty subsystems;

    Remembering previously solved problems;

    Reusing or adapting the previously solved problem;

    If no previously solved problem is available, ruling out the least likely hypotheses;

    Generating an initial hypothesis and assumptions about the problem;

    Testing this hypothesis based on domain knowledge;

    Interpreting the results of the test;

    Confirming or rejecting the validity of the hypothesis, and if it is rejected, generating a new hypothesis;

    Repeating the process of generating and testing hypotheses until the fault is identified.

- Implement the solution by replacing the defective part or subsystem.

    Test the solution to determine if the goal state is achieved.

- Record the results in a fault database (that is, remember the case for future reuse).

Case and System and Policy Analysis Problems

Case, system, or policy analysis problems (hereafter referred to as case problems) tend to be complex and ill-structured policy or analysis problems. Case analysis problems emerged at Harvard Law School nearly 130 years ago (Williams, 1992). Analyzing legal cases, preparing briefs, and defending judgments are authentic case analysis problems for law students. In business and many other professional contexts, such as international relations (Voss, Wolfe, Lawrence, and Engle, 1991) and managerial problem solving (Wagner, 1991), analyzing complex, situated case problems defines the nature of work. Business problems, including production planning, are common case problems. Classical situated case problems also exist in international relations, such as, "Given low crop productivity in the Soviet Union, how would the solver go about improving crop productivity if he or she served as Director of the Ministry of Agriculture in the Soviet Union?" (Voss and Post, 1988, p. 273). International relations problems involve situational analysis, decision making, solution generation, and testing in complex and dynamic political contexts.

Case and systems analysis problems are usually found everywhere except in the classroom, usually because they are complex and ill structured and therefore not amenable to easy assessment. Pick up any newspaper, and within the first few pages, you will find numerous case analysis problems:

- Where to locate a new municipal landfill

- How to develop a policy for rent control in Chicago

- How to pass a new funding law in a parliamentary country

- What to advise the president on political strategies in the Middle East

- How to resolve or at least mitigate racial prejudices in Malaysian schools

- How to encourage biodiversity in Third World countries

- What levels of farm subsidies to recommend in the Midwest

In addition to finding problems in newspapers or news magazines, you may wish to examine the Web site of the Union of International Associations (www.uia.org), an organization that maintains a database of thirty thousand problems around the world.

Case, system, or policy analysis problems are usually complex and interdisciplinary. That is, a reasonable solution is impossible by examining the problem from a single viewpoint. The problems set out in the list above all require economic, political, sociological, psychological, anthropological, and various scientific (engineering, chemical, biological) perspectives for their solution. Too often, case problems are insoluble because we focus too narrowly on situating the problem within a single domain. Is it a political, sociological, or economic problem? Likely it is all three.

In case analysis problems, goals are vaguely defined in the problem statement. Often, a significant part of the problem is understanding what the real problem is. No constraints may be stated, and little is known about how to solve the problem. There is usually no consensual agreement on what constitutes a good solution. The information available to the problem solver may be prodigious but may also be incomplete, inaccurate, or ambiguous (Voss, Wolfe, Lawrence, and Engle, 1991). Case analysis problems are very ill structured. Therefore, "the whole process of coping with a complex problem can be seen as a process of intention regulation" (Dörner and Wearing, 1995), that is, deciding what needs to be done. To complicate case analysis problems, "there are no formal procedures or guidelines to govern case analysis or evaluation of problem solutions," and what skilled performers need to know in order to solve these complex case problems is often tacit (Wagner, 1991, p. 179).

Solving case analysis problems cannot be as clearly defined as story problem solving or troubleshooting because the problems are ill structured. Bardach (2000) claims that solving policy problems is an eightfold process: define the problem, assemble some evidence, construct the alternatives, select the criteria, project the outcomes, confront the trade-offs, decide, and tell your story. Some of these activities are used for designing case analysis instruction. It is difficult to enumerate a process for case analysis problems; however, it generally starts with problem identification, followed by contextual analysis that involves a lot of information collection. When analyzing a complex situation, the problem solver intentionally seeks to identify the multiple personal, disciplinary, and thematic perspectives that may define the case. Who are the stakeholders, and what beliefs and perspectives do they bring to the case? The problem solver must also reconcile those perspectives into a solution; forecast outcomes (predicting effects); plan for implementation, which involves a lot of decision making; monitor the effects of one's actions; and reflect on the efficacy of the solution (Dörner and Wearing, 1995).

The final steps, implementation and assessment, are often impossible to accomplish in case problems. For example, it is not possible to try out a new political strategy on the Middle East and see what responses occur. Even if we could, the results could prove disastrous. Therefore, case analysis problems in education settings usually end with an argumentation stage. That is, the problem solvers will generate a solution and then argue for that solution (see Chapter Six). This process of justification provides valuable assessment information (see Chapter Eight). Sometimes it is the only form of assessment of problem-solving skills. Case analysis problems are among the most contextually dependent kind of problem solving, so analyzing cases places a much greater importance on situation analysis.

Why solve case analysis problems in schools or training situations, especially if they cannot be solved? Solving these problems is a lot more conceptually engaging than memorization. Solving case analysis problems engages learners in understanding and resolving the issues rather than remembering them. Resolving case analysis problems requires that learners critically analyze situations, identify issues and assumptions underlying different positions, consider consequences, use cognitive flexibility, and engage in reflective, ethical decision making (Lundeberg, 1999). These are all goals that educators espouse but too seldom engage in. Getting students to learn how to deal with ambiguity alone is a valuable goal in itself. Any teacher or professor who tires of students' asking what will be on the next test needs to engage his or her students in solving case, systems, or policy analysis problems. The levels of learning and thinking engaged by the process are at a much deeper level and are more meaningful. Although a quantifiable problem solution may not be possible, understanding the world or context that we live and function in helps us to construct much richer mental models of that world. If you are training business managers for international operations, for example, understanding the problems of the cultures in which they will operate will improve their abilities to manage. Many educational mission statements cite the importance of students' becoming better informed and more engaged citizens. Solving case analysis problems will help students to achieve that mission.

SUMMARY

Almost all learning in everyday and professional contexts (what some people refer to as the real world) is driven by the need to solve a problem, whether you admit it or not. Those who are better able to learn in order to solve problems have been more successful throughout history. Cave dwellers had to solve problems in order to survive environmental threats. Egyptians solved some very complex problems in order to build the pyramids. Wars throughout history can be viewed as problem-solving contests. In modern business, the best problem solvers dominate markets. Engineers, builders, marketers, chemists, politicians, social workers, and maintenance workers are paid to solve problems. In contemporary homes, the best problem solvers lead the most fulfilled lives. Problem solving is a major part of our everyday experience, and it is found everywhere *except* in schools, universities, and training organizations. When I have made this point to teachers, university faculty, and corporate trainers around the world, their reactions have varied from uneasiness to hostility. Perhaps they perceive problems as mysterious, confrontational, or impossible. Perhaps they do not know how to solve problems themselves. It is time that they learned.

If solving problems is the predominant intellectual skill required by workers and people in nearly every setting in the world (several corporate and institutional reports have made that claim), instructional designers should be developing models and methods for helping learners to become more effective problem solvers. When we lecture to students or trainees, we may feel good about what we have taught, but you can bet that the learners have learned (that is, made meaning of) little, if anything. Requiring students to memorize information for a test insults the learners and prevents them from becoming intellectually capable thinkers. When we learn something in the context of solving a problem, we understand and remember it better. If instructional designers do not begin to include problem solving as part of their instruction to students and trainees, then they are wasting their own time and students' time. In order to engage students in problem solving, we do not have to give them the basics before they can solve problems, for two reasons: first, we cannot give knowledge, and second, it is wishful thinking to hope that learners can take the basics and learn to solve problems when we have neither taught them nor even given them the opportunity. As educators and trainers, we have an obligation. We need to get started.

This book seeks to disseminate what I have learned about problem solving. It is only a beginning. There is so much more to learn. I hope that it helps you to confront some of your instructional problems.

2

Designing Learning Environments to Support Problem Solving

IN CHAPTER ONE, I listed a range of types of problems, noting that each type of problem solving requires a distinct combination of cognitive skills to solve. Therefore, each type of problem requires a distinct combination of instructional strategies and interactions to learn how to solve. At the end of Chapter One, I described three kinds of problems: story problems, troubleshooting, and case and systems analysis problems. Those descriptions included a model for how learners solve each kind of problem.

In this chapter, I describe models for designing instruction to support learning how to solve each kind of problem. These models describe the system components, the activities, and, to a limited extent, the sequences of interactions with those components and activities necessary for learning how to solve each kind of problem. These models can function as architectures for designing and developing learning environments to support each kind of problem solving. These models are based on theoretical and empirical research but have not themselves been evaluated. Research evaluating these models is ongoing.

Story Problems

The predominant method for teaching and solving story problems is the procedure of translating stories into formulas and then solving for the unknown. Students can become skilled at representing problems quantitatively without understanding the underlying principles represented by the formulas. "For years, physics professor Eric Mazur was confident that the students in his Harvard University introductory physics course were grasping the subject; after all, they excelled on . . . difficult quantitative exam problems" (Panitz, 1998, p. 17). When he gave them a test designed to assess their basic understanding of the physics concepts represented in the problems, "he was shocked by the dismal results. Apparently, many students had merely memorized equations and problem solving procedures without understanding the concepts behind them" (p. 17). This result invariably occurs when students use a "plug-and-chug" (plug values into formulas and chug to the solution) approach to solving story problems because plugging and chugging does not engage skills such as interpreting concepts or generating problem representations that are necessary for meaningful learning (Johnson, 2001). Every kind of problem solving requires that learners construct some sort of a mental model of the problem and base their solution plans on their model. It is important that learners demonstrate conceptual understanding of the problem before selecting a formula (Reusser, 1993).

In the following section, I describe a model for creating learning environments that help students learn to solve story problems conceptually and quantitatively. I describe each of the components and provide a brief description of how story-problem learning environments work.

Problem Type and Typology

The construction of a conceptual model of problems being solved is difficult because every different kind of problem has a different kind of model. As I showed in Chapter One, there are different kinds of the classic motion problems in math, such as overtake, opposite direction, round trip (a vehicle travels from point A to B and returns), and closure. Each kind of motion problem has a different set of structural relations between the entities that call on different processing operations.

It is essential that learners construct conceptual models that indicate comprehension of the relationships between the entities stated in the problem. Students must therefore learn about the structures of each class of problems that they are learning to solve. Classifying problem types by learners is essential to the understanding and transfer of problem solving (Mayer, Larkin, and Kadane, 1984). The reason is that novice learners tend to classify problems based on their surface content (the situational entities stated in the problem) rather than relationships embedded in the principles, resulting in a miscategorization of the problem type (Blessing and Ross, 1996). Classifying problems is important because as Mayer, Larkin, and Kadane (1984) found, learners more frequently commit errors when they miscategorize problems.

In nearly every domain that uses story problems, researchers have developed problem typologies. Even the simplest elementary mathematics story problems can be classified as change, compare, and combine problems (Riley and Greeno, 1988). A compare problem with the unknown as the amount of change would look like this:

Tom has four apples. Mary has some apples. Altogether, they have nine apples. How many apples does Mary have?

Mayer (1982) analyzed thousands of problems in high school algebra books for their structural similarities and identified eight families of story problems: amount per time rate, unit cost rate, percent cost rate, straight rate, geometry (simple area), physics (Ohm's law), statistics (combinations), and number stories. Within each family of story problems, Mayer identified categories of problems. For example, in amount per time rate problems, he identified motion problems, current problems, and work problems. Under each of these categories, he identified problem templates that share similar problem characteristics. For example, under motion problems, he identified templates such as overtake, opposite direction, round trip, closure, speed change, and same direction. The structure for motion-overtake problems specifies that "one vehicle starts and is followed later by a second vehicle that travels over the same route at a faster rate" (p. 156). In order to teach students how to solve story problems in any domain, a similar typology of problem types must be constructed in order to teach structural similarities and differences between problems.

In designing and developing computer-based story-problem learning environments in introductory physics, we constructed the problem typology shown in Figure 2–1. That graphic organizer is used to structure the learning

Figure 2–1. Graphical Organizer of Physics Problems.

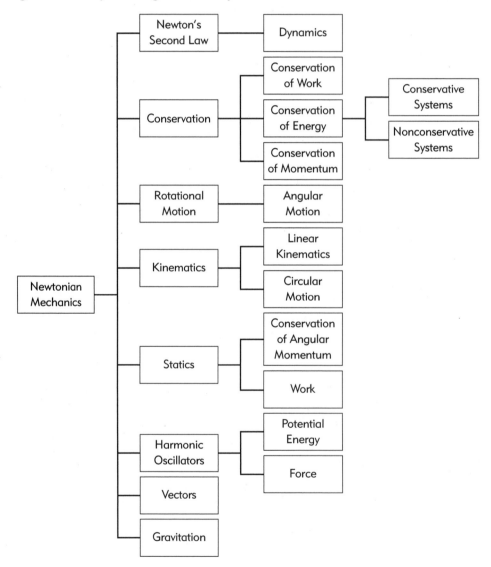

environment. When encountering the problem, the student must first use this typology to classify the present problem. Double-clicking on each problem type brings up examples of each problem type and the underlying physics principles. Emphasizing the structural properties of problems and contrasting them with other problems in the domain improves learners' abilities to generalize problems within the class and discriminate among classes based on the structural properties of the problem rather than surface-level, situational characteristics (Chi, Feltovich, and Glaser, 1981; Silver, 1981).

The structure of a story problem–solving environment (SPSE) is illustrated in Figure 2–2. I describe each of the components of the environment next.

Figure 2–2. Structure of the Story Problem–Solving Environment.

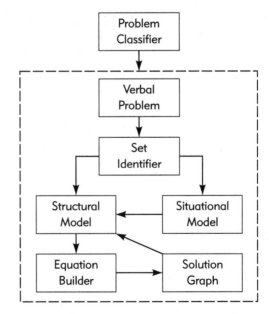

Problem Classifier. When working in the SPSE (illustrated in Figure 2–3), learners first have to select the problem type they believe describes the problem by using the pull-down menu in the upper left side of the screen. In this case, the learner correctly uses the Problem Classifier to select Kinematics, then Constant Velocity, and then 2-Dimensional.

Figure 2–3. Story Problem–Solving Environment in Physics.

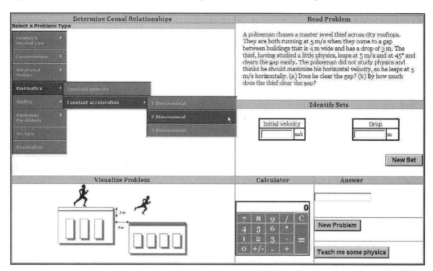

Verbal Problem. The student views the problem in the story problem–solving environment in the upper-right-hand corner of Figure 2–3. That is the problem
that was classified as a two-dimensional constant velocity problem. The problem always remains present in the upper-right-hand window to allow the student to look back and forth among representations.

Set Identifier. In order to build an internal problem representation, students must
construct an internal conceptual model of the problem. That model consists
of the relevant sets that comprise the problem. Parsing any story problem
requires that learners identify the sets that are important to the solution and
assign values to them (Briars and Larkin, 1984; Riley and Greeno, 1988).
Completing and assigning values to these propositions supports the construction of distinct models for each type of problem (Mayer, 1982).

In order to use the set identifier, the student highlights the entities and
their quantities in the verbal problem space in the upper-right corner of Figure 2–3 and drags each value from the problem into the Set Identifier. A set,
consisting of three smaller boxes, is automatically created. The student must
identify the object, the quantity, and the units describing the object. Three sets
have been identified in Figure 2–4: initial velocity, projectile angle, and drop.

Figure 2–4. Prototype of Physics Story Problem–Solving Environment.

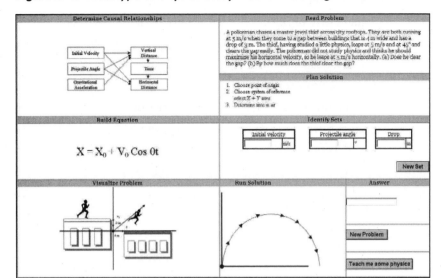

Structural Model. "A person who is working on physics problems must recognize the underlying structures of the problems, generate representations appropriate for discovering solutions, and make inferences on the generated representations" (Anzai, 1991, p 83). The underlying principles of physics, as with all other domains, are predicated on causal relationships among concepts. Each problem type in physics has a different structural model depicting a different combination of entities interrelated in unique ways. Having selected the problem type and identified the sets, the student drags and drops the sets from the Set Identifier onto the structural model (entitled Determine Causal Relationships in the upper left in Figure 2–4). The model describes the structural and causal components of the problem. While similar to the kinds of knowledge structures that Bagno, Eylon, and Ganiel (2000) used to demonstrate experts' knowledge structures, these models focus on describing the causal relationships between problem components. Students in this problem would drag initial velocity onto initial velocity, and so on. If students drag and drop a set onto the wrong element in the structural model, they receive explanatory feedback. Although this step may appear redundant, it emphasizes the conceptual relationships in the problem before mapping values onto formulas. Why is that important? Ploetzner, Fehse, Kneser, and Spada (1999) showed that when students and practitioners are solving physics problems, qualitative problem representations are necessary prerequisites to learning quantitative representations. Therefore, students should map problem values onto a qualitative (causal) representation of the problem before mapping the values onto a formula.

Another reason for mapping entities onto a structural model is that students rarely reconcile the situational model (story context) and structural model of the problem. In the SPSE, they are adjacent, allowing the student to compare and contrast the situational and structural models, which will provide for a richer mental model of the problem type. The most successful story-problem solvers are those who can integrate the situational and structural models of the story problems because both are important to problem solving.

Equation Builder. From the structural model, students assign values from the structural model onto an equation using the equation builder (Figure 2–4). In order to use the equation builder, the student drags values from the structural model into the equation space and then cancels out and reorganizes the variables. Once the student has completed the formula, he or she clicks a calculate button.

In order to test the accuracy of the values and the formula, an animated vector map plots the results in the Run Solution window. Nathan, Kintsch, and Young (1992) showed that students experiencing animated output outperformed students in nonanimated environments in recognizing a correct solution, generating equations from texts, and diagnosing errors.

Situation Model. Students need to view the situation model (called Visualize Problem in Figures 2–3 and 2–4). Although many psychologists believe that the surface content features of the problem distract learners from understanding the deep-level structure of the problem, others believe that effective problem solvers assemble quantitative constraints based on situational context (Briars and Larkin, 1984). Many quantitative models (formulas) easily map onto story structures. For example, compound motion and work problems have similar events, such as traveling in opposite directions, walking together, or riding a bus, with output and time as the basic dimensions that organize the story. Students make constructive inferences based on situational models. Blessing and Ross (1996) showed positive effects of situational content on problem solving and problem classification of experienced problem solvers (college students). Situational content is also valuable because it affects access to internal, mental problem schemas. Experts often base their categorizations on surface content (Novick, 1988).

When the student is solving the problem, the situational model overlays the system of reference over the visualization because of the importance in kinematics problems for determining the system of reference and it origin (Figure 2–4).

Worked Examples

Instruction consists of worked examples (described in detail in Chapter Five) using the SPSE environment to illustrate how to solve at least three problems for each problem type before allowing students to practice. Worked examples of problem solutions that precede practice improve practice-based problem solving by reducing the cognitive load and helping learners to construct problem-solving schemas (Cooper and Sweller, 1987; Sweller and Cooper, 1985).

In the SPSEs, an animated lifelike pedagogical agent (Lester, Stone, and Stelling, 1999; not shown in Figure 2–3 or 2–4) will work through at least two examples of each problem type. The agent first reads the verbal problem representation in the SPSE, looking for clues to help to classify the problem type. The agent then selects that problem type. The agent plans the solution by explicitly identifying the required subproblems. Clarifying the structure of subgoals in worked examples significantly improves performance (Atkinson, Derry, Renkl, and Wortham, 2000). The subproblems are added to the Plan Solution box as they are being performed—for example, (1) choose point of origin, (2) choose system of reference (x-axis and y-axis), (3) determine time in air (initial velocity plus how much it moved on y-axis), and (4) determine range of projectile motion on x-axis. The agent identifies the sets required for the problem in the set identifier, moves those sets into the structural model, and then maps those values into a formula in the equation builder. The agent performs a unit check and then estimates the size of the answer. The agent solves the formula and reconciles the outcome with the estimate. Performing this demonstration with two other more complex problems prepares the student for completing practice items.

Practice Items

Another essential component of any instruction is the opportunity to practice the skills acquired in the environment. Practice problems should be presented to students in the form that was illustrated in the worked examples, which should be similar to the form in which they are represented in the assessment. Students will be allowed to look back at the worked examples. They are fairly successful in matching practice problems with the examples, preferring the complex example as a model (Reed, Willis, and Guarino, 1994). Students will also be allowed to use the same SPSE interface that was used in the worked example in order to scaffold their practice performance. They will be allowed to use that scaffold until they are competent. Students will receive feedback during the practice sessions. If students identify the correct problem type, identify and place the correct problem sets into the correct problem representations, or make reasonable problem solution estimates, they will receive feedback about any of these activities.

Content Instruction

While classifying the problem type using the typology described in Figure 2–2 or at any time in the worked example or practice phases, the student can double-click on any of the components in the structural model and have the agent present conceptual instruction about the problem. In this environment, content instruction is provided on demand, using a just-in-time teaching approach (Novak, Patterson, Gavrin and Christianson, 1999).

Summary

A thorough review of the empirical and theoretical work on which this model is based is beyond the scope of this book. Other researchers have developed environments that fulfill some of these instructional functions contained in this model. For example, the Story Problem Solver (SPS) (Marshall, 1995) and the TiPS environment (Derry and TiPS Research Group, 2001) represent problems in structural models for displaying and solving arithmetic problems. These authors' assumption, like mine, is that qualitative problem representations are necessary prerequisites to learning quantitative representations (Ploetzner, Fehse, Kneser, and Spada, 1999). They also believe that problem structures vary among problem classes, and they have determined the procedures required to solve problem types. Other environments, for example, ANIMATE (Nathan, 1998), have represented the situational model of the problem through animations, mapping the animations onto a solution-enabling equation.

A number of attributes make the environment that I have described unique. No environment has attempted to integrate the structural and situational representations of the problem. Although SPS and TiPS require learners to identify the problem type, their selection process does not require the student to select from within a typology of problems. Also, the reasoning process required to solve story problems is embedded within the structure of the environment. Students must first classify the problem type, identify relevant sets from the problem representation, and map those sets onto a structural model before mapping the values onto a formula. Perhaps the greatest difference between this model and others is that it functions as a generic model for building on-line environments across subject domains. All other efforts have focused on individual problem types or small classes of problems. The purpose of the design model is to function as an architecture for on-line story-problem environments. Story problems in other domains can employ the same environment and structure as the one just described. The problems will differ, but the structure of the environment will be the same.

Troubleshooting Problems

Effective troubleshooting requires system knowledge, procedural knowledge, and strategic knowledge, and those kinds of knowledge are anchored to and organized by the troubleshooter's experiences. The most fundamental difference between expert and novice troubleshooters is their level of experience. Troubleshooting relies on experiential knowledge, which is exactly what novices lack. Experienced technicians through physicians index their knowledge around troubleshooting experiences. Often they can recall with extraordinary accuracy problems that they have troubleshot many years before. The problems that they most completely and accurately recall are those that were most difficult to solve, because the problem solver was more conceptually engaged by the process. Teaching novices to troubleshoot requires that they troubleshoot as many problems as possible in order to gain the experiential knowledge that will integrate the conceptual, procedural, and strategic knowledge that is required to troubleshoot.

Figure 2–5 illustrates a design model for building troubleshooting learning environments (TLEs) that integrate multiple kinds of knowledge required to troubleshoot. The model assumes that the most effective way to learn to troubleshoot is by troubleshooting problems. Learning to troubleshoot problems requires presenting learners with the symptoms of novel problems and requiring them to solve them. The major components of the TLE are a case library of previously solved problems, a troubleshooter that enables the learner to practice troubleshooting, and a rich conceptual model of the system being troubleshot. The conceptual model supports the construction of systems knowledge, the troubleshooter supports the construction of procedural and strategic knowledge, and the case library supports the construction of the experiential knowledge that integrates all of the other kinds of knowledge.

Figure 2–5. Model for Designing Troubleshooting Learning Environment.

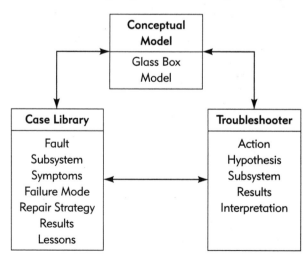

Conceptual Model

The troubleshooting environment is oriented by the conceptual model of the system being troubleshot. This model illustrates the interconnectedness of systems components. That is, what are all of the components and subsystems of the system in which the problem occurs, and how do they influence each other? Figure 2–6 illustrates a conceptual model of an automotive electrical system that was included in some problem-solving software produced by PLATO. When troubleshooting a car that will not start, the mechanic will not resort to trial and error, serial elimination, or other weak troubleshooting strategies, because he or she knows how the automotive electrical system works. That is, this person understands the function of each of

Figure 2–6. Systems Model for Troubleshooting Automotive Electrical System.

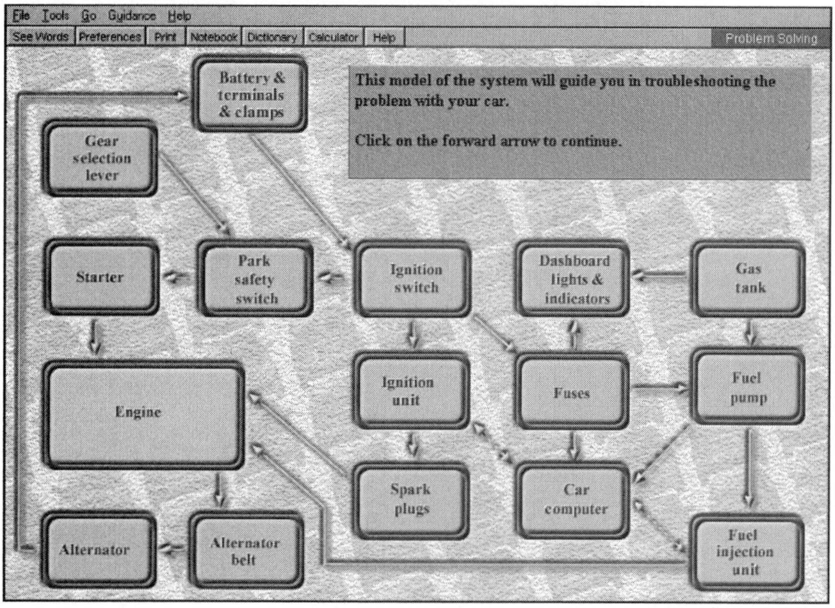

Source: Implemented in the Problem-Solving Experience from PLATO Corporation.

the components illustrated in Figure 2–6 and how they influence each other. The novice may not understand all of the components or their interactions and so may access instruction about each by clicking on the component. Conceptual understanding of the system is essential for troubleshooting. The illustration in Figure 2–6 is also used as an interface for predicting which component may be at fault.

Troubleshooter

The heart of the TLE is the troubleshooter (see Figure 2–7). This is where the learner acts like an experienced troubleshooter by troubleshooting new cases. After listening to a story about the automotive problem that describes the symptoms just before the car ceased to work, the learner (like an experienced troubleshooter) selects an action using the pull-down menu at the left of the screen, such as ordering a test, checking a connection, or trying a repair strategy. The novice may be coached about what action based on the symptomology to take first or may be free to select any action. Each action the troubleshooter takes shows up in the systems model. For each action the learner takes, the troubleshooter next requires the learner to state or select a fault hypothesis that she is testing using the pull-down menu to the right of the action menu. This is an implicit form of argumentation requiring the learner to justify the action taken (see Chapter Six for more detail on argumentation). If the hypothesis is inconsistent with the action, then feedback can be immediately provided about the rationale for taking such an action. Next, the learner must identify the subsystem in which the fault occurs. If the subsystem is inconsistent with the action, the learner is immediately sent to the conceptual model to better understand the workings of the subsystem that leads to the action or hypothesis. The learner then receives the result of action (for example, test results or system information) to the right of the subsystem and must interpret those results using the pull-down menu at the right of the troubleshooter. If the interpretation is inconsistent with the action, hypothesis, or subsystem, an error message is triggered. The error checking uses a very simple evaluation system.

Figure 2–7. Troubleshooter Architecture.

Trouble Shooter					Cases
Action	Subsystem	Hypothesis	Result	Interpretation	Case 1. Battery discharge 1
Test battery output					Case 2. Battery discharge 2
Check battery cable					Case 3. Battery failure 1
Test lights operating					
Test solenoid input					Case 4. Battery failure 2
Test solenoid output					Case 5. Starter failure 1
Test starter input					Case 6. Starter failure 2
Check					Case 7. Alternator failure
					Case 8. Generator fault 1
					Case 9. Ground fault 1
					Case 10. Ground fault 2
					Case 11. Cable fault 1
					Case 12. Solenoid failure 1
					Case 13. Solenoid failure 2

The troubleshooter (see Figure 2–7) requires the learner to think and act like an experienced troubleshooter. The environment integrates the troubleshooting actions, knowledge types (conceptual, strategic, and procedural), and conceptual systems model with a database of faults that have occurred with the system that the learner and others have solved. Initial instruction in how to use the system is provided by worked examples. As learners solve troubleshooting problems, the results of their practice cases can be added to their own case library of fault situations, so that they can learn from their personal experience.

At any moment during the learning process, the learner may access just-in-time instruction about how to perform the action (for example, an electronic test or checking symptoms) or the multimodal results from such activities. Jonassen and Henning (1999) showed that refrigeration technicians often rely on different modalities when conversing with machines and tools. They regularly place their hands on pipes to sense temperatures, listen to the sound of a compressor, look for oil stains on the floor, or interact with the computer screen. They communicate through sense impressions—what one technician refers to as "touchy-feely" knowledge.

Case Library

If the troubleshooter is the heart of the TLE, the case library is the head (memory) of the TLE. Discourse is essential to negotiating problems, solutions, or meaning. In troubleshooting situations in everyday contexts, the primary medium of negotiation is stories. When a troubleshooter experiences a problem, she most often describes the problem to someone else, who recalls from memory a similar problem and tells the troubleshooter about the recalled experience. These stories provide contextual information, work as a format for diagnosis, and also express an identity among participants in any kind of community. Stories about how experienced troubleshooters have solved similar troubleshooting problems are contained in, indexed by, and made available to learners in a case library (also known as a *fault database*).

The case library, or fault database, contains stories of as many troubleshooting experiences as possible. Each case represents a story of a domain-specific troubleshooting instance. Case libraries, based on principles of case-based reasoning, represent the most powerful form of instructional support for ill-structured problems such as troubleshooting (Jonassen and Hernandez-Serrano, 2002). The case library indexes each case or story according to its system fault, the system or subsystem in which the fault occurred, or the symptoms of the fault, similar to the troubleshooter. The failure mode, hypotheses, or strategies that were tested, the results of those tests, and what lessons were learned from the experience are also contained in the case library.

The case library represents the experiential knowledge of potentially hundreds of experienced troubleshooters because troubleshooters almost invariably store their knowledge of problems and solutions in terms of their experiences. The best troubleshooters are the most experienced ones. That experiential knowledge is precisely what learners do not possess. A learner who encounters any difficulty or is uncertain about how to proceed may access the case library to learn about similar cases, what was done, and what the results were. The TLE can also be programmed to access a relevant story automatically when a learner commits an error, orders an inappropriate test, or takes some other action that indicates a lack of understanding. Stories are easily collected from experienced troubleshooters by presenting them with a problem and asking them if they are reminded of a similar problem that they have solved. Invariably they are.

Hernandez-Serrano and Jonassen (2003) showed that access to a case library during learning how to solve problems improved complex problem-solving performance on an examination. Case libraries and case-based reasoning are explained in greater detail in Chapter Five.

Worked Examples

Similar to learning how to solve story problems, learners will be introduced to the troubleshooter, case library, and conceptual model through worked examples that illustrate not only how to use the TLE but also model different troubleshooting strategies (for example, space splitting, in order to isolate the faulty subsystem before conducting any tests). If the TLE is entirely on-line, an animated lifelike pedagogical agent (Lester, Stone, and Stelling, 1999) will work through at least two examples of each problem type. The agent reads the problem representation in the TLE, modeling strategies such as looking for clues and rejecting the least likely hypothesis, before using the troubleshooter. The agent also models how to gain the most benefit from the conceptual model and case library.

Practice Items

Practice consists of using the troubleshooter to troubleshoot new problems. During practice, new problems are presented to the learner, who uses the troubleshooter to isolate the cause of the problem. The learner may access the conceptual model or case library at will. How many practice problems are required to develop different levels of troubleshooting skill depends on the complexity of the system being troubleshot, the abilities and dispositions of the learners, and a host of other factors.

It is worth noting that every action that learners take during their practice (actions in the troubleshooter, accessing information in the conceptual model, or accessing cases from the case library) can be used to assess their understanding and troubleshooting skills. The purpose of that assessment may be to track progress during learning or merely to see if the learner is mindfully engaged in the learning process. Assessment processes are described in more detail in Chapter Eight.

Case, Systems, or Policy Analysis Problems

Case, system, or policy analysis problems (hereafter referred to as case problems) are complex, ambiguous, and very ill structured. As such, they represent the antithesis of most formal education, which focuses on correct answers and finding truth. Analyzing and trying to solve these problems is challenging for most learners, from kindergartners through adults, for several reasons. Students' scripts for "doing school" possess well-established routines. The teacher or professor or trainer tells the students what they should know, and the students attempt to know it. The teacher, professor, or trainer then assesses how well the students know it. However, case analysis problems often present unknowable phenomena that must be socially negotiated and co-constructed. There never is a single perspective that represents the truth. Solving these problems requires that students accommodate ambiguity, but tolerance for ambiguity is low among teachers and students. Why? It has to do with their epistemic beliefs, that is, what we believe that knowledge, truth, and learning mean. People develop their beliefs from simple black-and-white thinking, through an exploration of multiple perspectives, to complex, relativistic thinking.

The epistemological foundation for most education is what Baxter-Magolda (1987) calls absolute knowing, where individuals believe that knowledge and truth are certain and should be obtained from authorities. Solving case problems requires transitional knowing (knowledge is partially certain and requires understanding using logic, debate, and research), independent knowing (knowledge is uncertain and requires independent thinking and open-mindedness), and contextual knowing (knowledge is based on evidence in context). Students are most commonly absolute thinkers and find case problems very challenging because there is no correct answer. However, if students never face ill-structured case problems, they probably will never develop independent or contextual thinking skills. Exposure to ambiguity represents a learning experience.

Figure 2–8 illustrates a model for designing a case analysis learning environment. We will look at each of these components.

Figure 2–8. Model for Case and System Analysis Problem-Solving Environment.

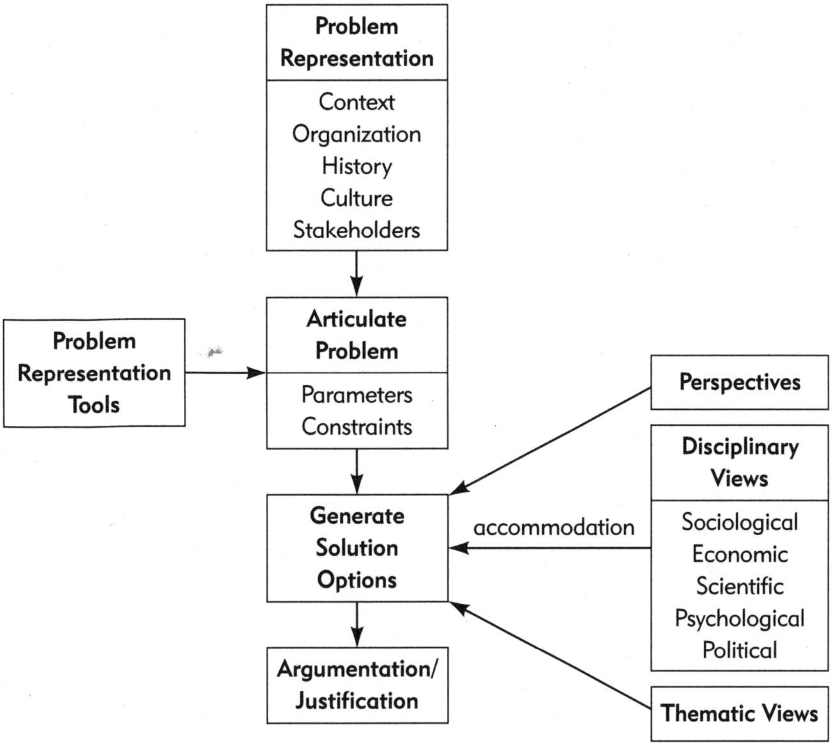

```
                          ┌─────────────────────┐
                          │       Problem       │
                          │   Representation     │
                          ├─────────────────────┤
                          │      Context         │
                          │   Organization       │
                          │      History         │
                          │      Culture         │
                          │    Stakeholders      │
                          └─────────────────────┘
                                     │
                                     ▼
┌──────────────────┐      ┌─────────────────────┐
│     Problem       │      │     Articulate       │          ┌──────────────────┐
│  Representation   │─────▶│      Problem         │          │   Perspectives    │
│      Tools        │      ├─────────────────────┤          └──────────────────┘
└──────────────────┘      │    Parameters        │          ┌──────────────────┐
                          │    Constraints       │          │   Disciplinary    │
                          └─────────────────────┘          │      Views        │
                                     │                      ├──────────────────┤
                                     ▼                      │   Sociological    │
                          ┌─────────────────────┐  accommo- │    Economic       │
                          │      Generate        │◀─dation──│    Scientific     │
                          │      Solution        │          │   Psychological   │
                          │      Options         │          │     Political     │
                          └─────────────────────┘          └──────────────────┘
                                     │                      ┌──────────────────┐
                                     ▼                      │  Thematic Views   │
                          ┌─────────────────────┐          └──────────────────┘
                          │   Argumentation/     │
                          │   Justification      │
                          └─────────────────────┘
```

Problem Presentation

Because case analysis problems (like all other ill-structured problems) are more context dependent than well-structured problems, it is necessary to develop a more authentic and situated task environment (Voss and Post, 1988). If case analysis thinking is determined largely by the context and the domain that it represents, it is important to describe the social, political, and organizational context of the problem adequately. Therefore, a context analysis needs to be conducted. What is the nature of the domain? What are the constraints imposed by the context? What kinds of problems are solved in this domain, and, equally important, what are the contextual constraints that affect the problem? The problem should be evaluative, describing system breakdowns, dissatisfied people, the existence of discrimination, and so on.

Case analysis problems are often represented by stories (see Chapter Five for a detailed rationale for using stories). Stories are better understood, better remembered, and more empathic than didactic representations of problems. The following excerpt is taken from a case analysis learning environment that we developed on the sociology of welfare. This story introduces a problem in the welfare cycle (seeking assistance, support, welfare to work): how to help people through the welfare-to-work cycle. Another major goal of the environment was to invoke empathic responses from culturally isolated students at a large state university.

TUESDAY, FEBRUARY 2

My name's Tiffany. I'm on my way to Lewistown with my daughter, Stephanie. Stephanie's almost five, now. I had her when I was eighteen. My home and friends are in Detroit. I can't stay there no more. I got involved with a gang there, selling drugs and dealin'. It took me five years to realize that I didn't want to live like that no more. I was stealin' and doing things I never thought I would. I love my little girl. I realized I would be harmin' her if I stayed with them.

When you've done and seen what I have, there's no point in wanting "out" unless you're prepared to do it. So I'm leaving, with no cash, no help from no-one. Just Stef and me. Yeah, this has been my "Happy Christmas." I'm lookin' for my natural mother. I know she lived in Lewiston, Pennsylvania, when I was born. It's a long shot, though. I have an address for her for 1992. I aint never met her. She don't know I'm comin'. I have nowhere else to go—just can't stay in Detroit—no way. I'm near eight months knocked up. I gotta get help, right away when I get there, for the sake of my babies.

WEDNESDAY, FEBRUARY 3 (5:30 P.M.)

Stephanie ain't never traveled on no Greyhound bus before. A twenty-hour ride has just about dimmed her enthusiasm—poor baby. Thank God she slept. We left the Howard Street station in Detroit at 10:00 last night and got here at 5:15 today. In this rotten weather, it'll be dark soon. We haven't eaten since we finished our snacks. Jeez, the smell from this Market Street Grill is drivin' me crazy. What have I done? My ticket was $59. That's crazy! Maybe I should o' kept my money.

I aint got no idea where to go here. The number I have for my mother ain't givin' me no answer. I only have three quarters for the phone. Thirty dollars and my kid and this ol' beach bag with Stef's clothes and Beanie Babies and some things for myself, that's all I have. And jeez, is this place small, and cold. I know I gotta find us some help. This number still ain't answering. There's no message. Maybe this isn't even the number. . . . It's gettin' late. What are we gonna do?

Representing case analysis problems in terms of stories is not enough to engage learners in the kind of thinking that is necessary for solving case problems. It is equally, if not more, important to provide students with a specific, authentic task to solve. In the social welfare problem just described, we required students to counsel this woman who was seeking to move from welfare to work. Their counseling not only had to be legally correct (the students became very frustrated by the complexity of the forms and the procedures that had to be completed by the recipients) but also empathic.

The task also needs to be fairly specific. The task for a foreign-policy analysis problem on the Middle East might require the students to act as foreign policy analysts for the U.S. State Department who are tasked with recommending specific policy actions to the secretary of state about whether Palestinians should be granted independent statehood. That is, there should be a specific kind of outcome (advice) associated with the task—not just a report but a report with specific action items. This does not mean that a particular kind of advice should be given, just the form of advice. A case analysis problem on the political system in

Norway should require recommendations about how to build a parliamentary coalition necessary to pass legislation approving the construction of a gas-fired electrical plant. The more purposeful the task is, the more engaging it will be.

The same environment with all of its support systems may be altered by redefining the task. Some students may be assigned to an environment that seeks to build a coalition to block the construction of a gas-fired electrical plant. Except for the task, the remainder of the environment may be the same or very similar. In another environment designed for a geography course focusing on the use of maps (Figure 2–9), we awarded students a contract from the state Department of Transportation to select an alternate route to bypass a disastrously designed highway intersection.

Figure 2–9. Traffic Problem.

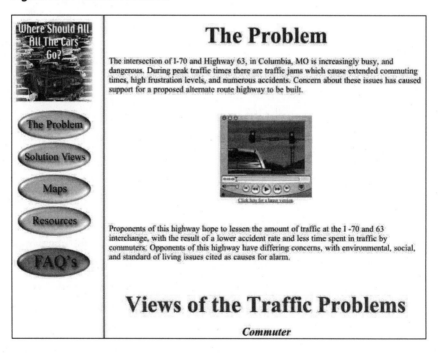

The students had to accommodate the views of motorist, merchants, homeowners, and bureaucrats while using soil, topographic, aerial, and parcel maps to find the most efficient, effective, and acceptable solution to the problem. Needless to say, no absolutely correct solutions exist, only better and worse solutions.

The task should be as real as possible, and it should be fairly well circumscribed. Too often, problem-solving attempts in the classroom fail because the task is too diffuse. Perhaps students are assigned to analyze policy or principles. If they do not perceive a meaningful purpose for the problem-solving activity, they are not likely to buy into the problems or their solutions.

Problem Representation Tools

I have described ways that the problem can be represented to the students, including narrative format and concise, authentic tasks. It is important to note that the ways that we represent problems to learners in the problem statement affects how problem solvers mentally represent the problems that they are trying to solve. That is the goal: to get learners to construct a meaningful conceptual model of the problems they are trying to solve. However, problem representation is only one source of influence.

The model for engaging learners in case analysis problems calls for their use of tools to construct their own external representation of the problems. The systems dynamics model of the smoking population in Figure 2–10 represents the kind of problem representation tools that can be used to represent case analysis problems. This model (produced with a systems modeling tool called Stella) depicts the dynamic relationships among the factors affecting the population. If the task was to reduce smoking in the U.S. population in order to reduce health care costs, the students might begin by building such a model. Systems dynamics tools enable learners to add or subtract factors and test the effects of changes in those factors. These tools also enable the students to test their models by changing parameter values and noticing the effects.

Figure 2–11 shows the output of the model when additional antismoking campaign money is contributed. The outcomes of such models may also be used as data to support student arguments. Chapter Four has a more extensive treatment of the use of problem representation tools.

Figure 2–10. Systems Dynamics Model of the Smoking Population.

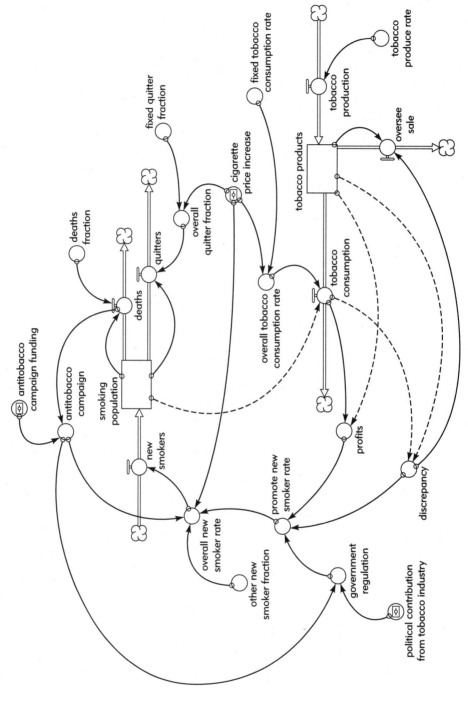

Figure 2–11. Output of the Systems Dynamics Model.

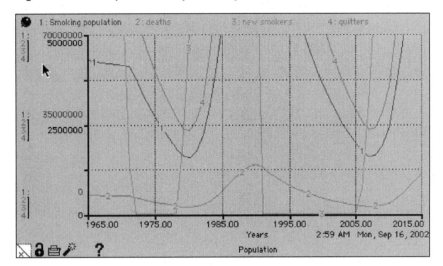

Generate Solution Options: Accommodating Multiple Perspectives. Bardach (2000) suggests assembling evidence as a second step. Evidence defines the problem and enables learning to assess policies. It is important to provide divergent and even contradictory evidence. One of the best models for facilitating the consideration different kinds of evidence, an essential process for solving case analysis problems and becoming an epistemically mature leaner, is cognitive flexibility theory (Spiro and Jehng, 1990). Cognitive flexibility theory stresses the conceptual interrelatedness of ideas and their interconnectedness. Cognitive flexibility environments intentionally represent multiple perspectives or interpretations of the content in the cases that are used to illustrate the content domain. The ill-structuredness of any knowledge domain is best illustrated by multiple perspectives or themes that are inherent in the problems that are represented.

We used a cognitive flexibility hypertext in an environment on issues of biodiversity, land use, and control and conflict resolution styles as they have emerged in the controversy surrounding the reintroduction of the Mexican gray wolf into wilderness areas of the American Southwest. The wolf reintroduction environment (see Figure 2–12) allows the learner to examine the

Figure 2–12. Wolf Reintroduction Environment.

Reintroduction of the Wolf into the Southwest

Long before cowboys roamed, before Spaniards rode in conquest, before even the Apache and Navajo arrived, wolves inhabited the ancient Southwest, but as cattle ranching took hold in the 1800s, the predatory wolf became an obstacle to commerce. By the 1920s it was just about exterminated from the Western landscape. But wolves are making a comeback of a kind in part because of shifting public values.

In January 1995, 19 Canadian gray wolves were released into Yellowstone National Park by the U.S. Fish and Wildlife Service. In January 1996 another 20 were brought to Yellowstone and to Idaho, and in early 1997 the Southwest will get its share. Mexican gray wolves are scheduled to be reintroduced into the wilderness of Arizona and New Mexico, but the battle for public acceptance is still being waged. Should the Mexican wolf be reintroduced? You decide.

For more information, you can read this piece by Sandy Tolan of National Public Radio's Weekend Edition.

To help you make up your mind, you can listen to several people in the area who would be affected by the re-introduction:

- Al Schneeberger of the New Mexico Cattle Growers Association
- A Woman of Catron County
- Man in the Field Interviews
- Charmin Russel
- Dutch Salmon, publisher of High Lonesome Books
- Jim Cook
- Pamela Brown
- The Holders

You can think about some of the major issues involved.

- Consumption vs. Conservation
- Confrontation vs. Cooperation
- National control vs. Local control

reintroduction issue from the perspectives of a dozen or so people who are affected by the wolves, including ranchers and environmentalists. We also identified various thematic issues interwoven through their comments, including local versus national control of the land, consumption versus conservation, and cooperation versus co-optation. In order to render a judgment on the continuation of the practice, students had to understand and accommodate these viewpoints. It is essential that students understand the different perspectives that make case analysis problems complex in order to generate and evaluate different solutions.

Argumentation/Justification. Ill-structured problems are dialectical in nature: two or more opposing conceptualizations of the problem (different problem spaces) are used to support different arguments with opposing assumptions underlying them (Churchman, 1971). Although Bardach (2000) suggests contrasting alternative solutions for learners to evaluate, I believe that it is important that learners are able to articulate the differing assumptions in support of arguments for whatever solution that they recommend. The argument provides the best evidence for domain knowledge that they have acquired. Developing cogent arguments to support divergent thinking (or reflective judgment; Kitchner and King, 1981) engages not only cognition and metacognition of the processes used to solve the problem but also awareness of the epistemic nature of the process and the truth or value of different solutions (Kitchner, 1983). In the geography environment, there are many possible routes that can be chosen and many possible reasons for choosing any one of them. Requiring students to develop an argument for their choice is tantamount to problem solving. It provides very useful assessment data to help the teacher determine what and how much the learners know. Coaching or prompting can be provided in the form of a series of reflective judgment prompts or questions (Kitchner and King, 1981)—for example:

- Can you ever know for sure that your position is correct? Will we ever know which is the correct position?

- How did you come to hold that point of view? On what do you base it?

- When people differ about matters such as this, is it ever the case that one is right and the other wrong or that one opinion is worse and the other better?

- How is it possible that people can have such different points of view?

- What does it mean to you when the experts disagree on this issue?

SUMMARY

In this chapter, I have explored models and methods for designing problem-based learning environments to help students learn how to solve story problems, troubleshooting problems, and case, systems, or policy analysis problems. These are three distinct kinds of problems that can be solved in classrooms from kindergarten through graduate school. They are also fairly generic models that can accommodate domain-specific and context-specific knowledge structures and intellectual requirements. In the next three chapters, I explore more fully most of the components contained in the design models described in this chapter.

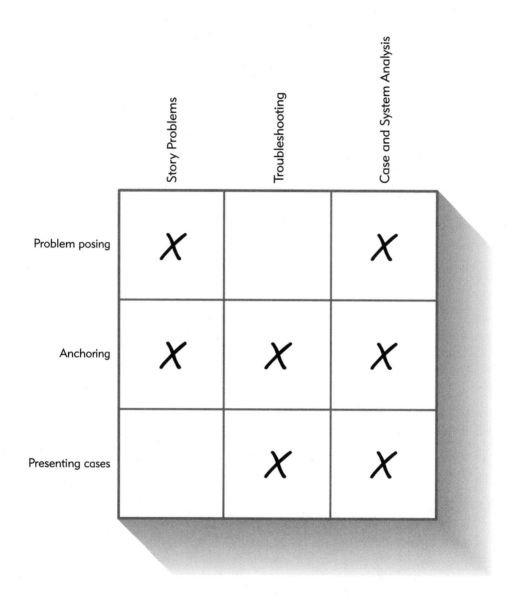

Figure 3–1. Methods for Presenting Problems to Learners by Problem Type.

3

Presenting Problems to Learners

THE WAY THAT problems are presented to learners can substantially influence how the problems are understood and solved, according to cognitive research in the 1970s and 1980s. Well-structured (textbook) problems, for example, are typically presented to learners in text form. Learners must interpret the text and encode problem information in whatever internal representational form that they use. At the other end of the representational spectrum, newer situated and authentic forms of instruction, such as anchored instruction, insist on rich and realistic video for presenting problems to learners (Cognition and Technology Group at Vanderbilt, 1992).

Why is the way that we represent problems to learners important? The assumption is that the attributes of external problem representations will be mapped onto learners' mental representations. Organizing and displaying problems to learners in ways that develop their mental representations and engage appropriate problem-solving processes is the goal. For example, for story problems, matrix representations of information were substantially superior to groupings, graphs, and sentences because they clearly define needed information, suggest orders of operations, and provide consistency checks for partial solutions (Schwartz, 1971; Schwartz and Fattaleh, 1973). Presenting problems in diagrams has also helped learners solve problems better than presenting problems as verbal representations, especially for more complex problems (Mayer, 1976).

It appears that form, organization, and sequence of problem representation affect cognitive processes during problem solving. Zhang (1997) argues that the form of the external representation of problems determines what information can be perceived, what processes can be activated, and what structures can be discovered from the representation. That is, external representations are more than merely inputs to internal representation processes during problem solving. It is important to note that these differences in cognitive processing have been found only for well-structured story problems. No research on how problem representation affects complex, ambiguous, and ill-structured problems exists. It is likely that representational differences have greater effects on ill-structured problems because of their difficulty. Based on related research and theory, I recommend three methods for representing different problems that should positively affect different kinds of problems as illustrated in the matrix in Figure 3–1 (see page 46): problem posing, anchored instruction, and case-based presentations.

Problem Posing

Well-structured problems normally are expected to result in well-structured answers. That is the nature of well-structured problems. When we ask students to solve $x^2 + y^2 = z^2$, students will necessarily want to substitute values like 3, 4, and 5 to solve the problem. In a wonderful little book, *The Art of Problem Posing* (1990), Brown and Walter argue that $x^2 + y^2 = z^2$ is not a question at all. Rather, it begs the learner to ask a question or pose a problem. How do you do that? Start by making observations, asking questions, or making conjectures about the formula. It is the Pythagorean theorem. What if it were not a theorem? What could it be? It defines right triangles. How do we know that it is true? And so on.

Problem posing assumes that there are many ways of thinking about problems other than getting the right answer. Brown and Walter (1990) argue, "It is extremely important mathematically as well as intellectually to appreciate that there are times not only when it is unnecessary and undesirable to get exact answers" (p. 25). Why are we so compelled to find exact answers? Curriculum developers define curriculum in terms of subject matter content. In mathematics and the sciences, that content consists of laws, theorems, and definitions. Geometry instruction, for example, almost always begins with axioms—for example, "The shortest distance between two points is the length of the line segment connecting those points."

Rather than asking math and science students to solve a formula, Brown and Walter suggest posing questions such as these:

- What purpose does the formula serve?
- What is the number of objects or cases satisfying this condition?
- What is the range of the answer?
- What is the pattern in this case?
- Is there a counterexample?
- Is there a solution?
- Can I find it?
- Can I prove it?
- When is it false? When true?
- Is there a limiting case?
- Is there a uniting theme?
- What does it remind me of?
- What do I need in order to prove it?
- What are the key features of the situation?
- What are the key constraints?

Such questions will be problematic to most students, who have been conditioned to search for the exact answer. Although the purpose of these diversionary questions may appear to be to confuse students, they are really trying to get students to develop conceptual understanding of the rules, theorems, and laws that are represented by formulas.

In Chapter Two, I related a story about Harvard University students who were victims of the same compulsion to get the exact answer. Brown and Walter (1990) believe that in order to get students to develop conceptual understanding, they must view the problem from different perspectives by asking different questions about it. In a sense, they are trying to make well-structured problems a little more ill structured. Why? Learning is an ill-structured phenomenon. Different students may all get the same answer, but the sense that each person makes of the problem will be different.

Anchoring Problems in Macrocontexts

One of the best-known and most effective innovations in instructional design is anchored instruction. Based on situated learning theory and cognitive apprenticeships, anchored instruction embeds problems into complex and realistic scenarios called *macrocontexts*. Developed by the Cognition and Technology Group at Vanderbilt (1992), anchored instruction uses high-quality video scenarios for introducing the problem and engaging learners in order to make the problems more motivating and easier to search. A video is used to present a story narrative that requires the learners to generate the problem to be solved rather than having the entire problem circumscribed by the instruction. All of the data needed to solve the math and science problems are embedded in the story, enabling students to make decisions about what data are important. The problems that students generate and solve are complex rather than simple story problems, and they often require more than twenty steps to solve.

The Cognition and Technology Group at Vanderbilt designed and developed two full series of video-based problems, "Adventures of Jasper Woodbury" and "Scientists in Action." "Adventures of Jasper Woodbury" consists of twelve videodisk-based adventures (plus video-based analogues, extensions, and teaching tips) that focus on mathematical problem finding and problem solving. Each adventure is designed from the perspective of the standards recommended by the National Council of Teachers of Mathematics. In particular, each adventure provides multiple opportunities for problem solving, reasoning, communication, and making connections to other areas, such as science, social studies, literature, and history.

In the geometry series for grades 5 and up, Paige Littlefield, a Native American, is following a set of clues to find a family heirloom her grandfather left for her in a cave. As Paige searches for the cave, we learn about topographic maps and concepts of geometry important for measurement. An accident occurs when Paige reaches the cave. Students must help her friend, Ryan, find the cave on a map and give directions for the Rescue Squad to get there as quickly as possible. Incorporating real-world map-reading skills with angle and linear measurement, this is a challenging episode for math and social studies.

In the series "Working Smart," teenagers Jasper, Emily, and Larry compete in a problem-solving contest sponsored by a local travel agency. They set about creating mathematical smart tools that will allow them to solve several classes of travel-related problems efficiently and quickly in hopes of winning an all-expenses-paid trip anywhere in the United States. All three episodes help students see the power of algebra, demonstrating that a mathematical representation can be created for a whole class of problems.

Using the same set of assumptions used to design the Jasper series, the "Young Scientist" series provides scientific adventures for students to solve. In the "Stones River Mystery," students in the field and in an electronically connected classroom have been monitoring a local river for pollution. During one sampling trip, they notice that the measures they are monitoring have begun to change. The students and scientists must work together to determine where the pollution is coming from. In "Lost Letters of Lazlo Clark," a time capsule has been found during a renovation of the local high school. In it are letters and a map from Lazlo Clark, a local philanthropist who had donated a large tract of land to the area almost a hundred years ago. Students and their science teacher set out to find some Native American petroglyphs mentioned in Clark's letters. Although their initial trip is not successful, it helps them understand the importance of planning to make such a trip and how much science is needed.

Anchored instruction has proved very successful in engaging students and getting them to solve problems more complex than their teachers thought possible. The basis of their success is student ownership of the problems.

Case-Based Instruction

Cases fulfill at least two roles in learning to solve problems: exemplars and representing problem situations (Carter, 1999). I believe that there is a third use of cases: to represent problems to learners to be solved.

First, cases can function as exemplars, exemplifying problem-solving practices in direct teaching. When teaching students about problem solving, you can show examples of different kinds of problems that vex practitioners. Second, cases can function as instructional support during problem-solving activities. When trying to solve a problem, you can show students how others have attempted to solve similar problems. This use is described in Chapter Five as case libraries. Third, cases can be used to represent problems to learners to be solved, that is, the case is the focus of instruction. That is the use described in this chapter.

The use of cases in instruction began at Harvard Law School in the 1870s, migrating later to many medical schools and later to business schools. Cases are most often conceived of as descriptions of problems that are presented to students to analyze and perhaps solve. Cases are valued because they simulate authentic activity that is situated in some real-world context. They usually simulate real problems that have occurred in business, law, medicine, teaching, and just about any other applied field.

What makes case-based instruction revolutionary is that teaching begins not with a theoretical exegesis of domain concepts but rather with a real problem. This may not seem radical on the face of it, but problem-first teaching is antithetical to hundreds of years of educational practice. Rather than learning (and forgetting) all about a field before being allowed to solve a meaningful problem, case-based instruction is based on the belief that what you learn while trying to solve a complex problem you will better comprehend and retain much longer. Williams (1992) asks a number of questions that easily demarcate case-based from traditional instruction:

- Does the instruction begin with a problem to be solved?
- Does the teacher model how to solve problems in the content of the presented problem?
- Do students actively engage in solving the problem?
- Do students and teacher assess how well learning is progressing?
- Are the problems authentic, like those solved by practitioners?
- Are the problems realistically complex?

The goal of using cases to represent problems is to make the case interesting and compelling enough that students will want to solve it. The more effort that students make to solve the problem, the more ownership they will have in its solution. The most important rationale for case-based instruction is that it at least simulates the kind of activity that students are preparing for. No one in the everyday world gets paid for memorizing facts and taking examinations. People are paid to solve problems, so we should start them off learning to solve problems. Next, I describe the components of problem cases and then methods for representing them.

Components of Case Problems

In order to be engaging, cases must convey several attributes of the problem, including an extensive description of the case context: descriptions of the performance environment, the stakeholders and their relationships with each other, and the problem. The learning environment, be it text, video, or computer based, should describe the physical, sociocultural, and organizational climate surrounding the problem. Where and in what time frame does it occur? What physical resources surround the problem? What is the nature of the business, agency, or institution in which the problem occurs? What do they produce? What is the organizational and sociocultural climate in the organization? Are there annual reports, mission statements, balance sheets, or profit-and-loss statements that can appropriately describe the situation? What is the history of the setting?

It is also important to describe the community of practice. Who are the players in the case? Who are the stakeholders, and what are their beliefs, biases, and purposes? What are the values, beliefs, sociocultural expectations, and customs of the people involved? Who sets policy? What sense of social or political efficacy do the members of the setting or organization feel? What are the skills and performance backgrounds of performers? Provide resumés for key players that describe not only their experience but also their hobbies, traits, and beliefs. You can also convey this information in stories or interviews with key personnel in the form of audio or video clips. It is the community of participants who define what problem-solving performance means in this context.

Case Format

The problem and problem context is usually represented as a story about a set of events that leads up to the problem that needs to be resolved. In these cases, characters are developed who interact in realistic ways to introduce the case problem. Williams (1992) asks whether problems are presented to learners in ways that make their complexity manageable, such as stories, presenting them on video, and organizing all required data. Stories are also the primary means of problem representation and coaching in goal-based scenarios (Lindeman and others, 1995).

Aggregate Planning. Aggregate planning is a process of balancing demand, technology, human resources, and inventory. Figure 3–2 shows the opening screen of a problem-based learning environment on aggregate planning: students are required to decide how many part-time and full-time employees to hire and fire in order to meet demand. Human resources represent the most important component of this tax accounting firm. Students must accommodate the reality that it costs money to hire and train employees as well as to fire employees.

The environment that we designed (Jonassen, Prevish, Christy, and Stavurlaki, 1999) opens with a story that establishes the context and the purpose of the environment. The student learns a little about the history of the firm, its general operations, and its goals. Students can access financial information about the company, its demand and sales, and other important aspects before beginning to make the complex aggregate planning decisions. The story ends where Bernard takes control of the firm and has to make hiring and firing decisions aided by a spreadsheet with costs built in.

Figure 3–2. Presenting the Problem in an Aggregate Planning Environment.

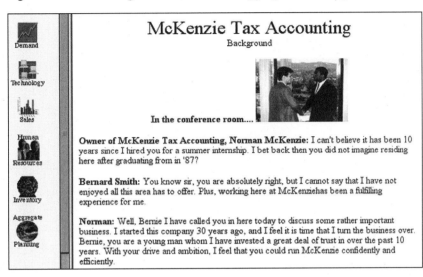

Global Trends. As part of a course on global trends, we developed a case (policy) analysis learning environment where students had to advise the president on hot spots throughout the world. One of the hot spots is Kosovo. Following a briefing on the subject, an extensive panel of experts (see Figure 3–3) has generated a number of options for dealing with the following task:

In light of the upcoming U.S. presidential elections, the president has called for a review of policy options for the future of Kosovo. These policy options were laid out months ago in preparation for the outcome of this conflict.

Option 1: Declare Kosovo an interim international protectorate.

Option 2: Establish Kosovo as an independent state.

Option 3: Negotiate with Serbia conditions for the partition of Kosovo with some parts to fall under Kosovar Albanian rule, and some parts under Yugoslavian rule.

Option 4: Make Kosovo part of a greater Albania.

The president has asked for a review of these policies in light of the current situation, and wants to see the pros and cons of each policy option laid out. The president would also like to see implementation issues laid out for the option the committee has decided on.

Figure 3–3. Kosovo Liberation Presentation.

In addition to the briefing, we assembled a committee of experts that can be queried. During the committee meeting, the student can get reports from any of the agencies listed in the left frame of Figure 3–4. Clicking on CIA brings up a report from the CIA director (Figure 3–4).

In this environment, we tried to simulate the ambiguity of the real-world problem environment. We presented a problem and different perspectives and positions on the problem, which is consistent with the way that international relations problems occur.

SUMMARY

The ways that problems are represented to learners affects the ways that learners understand them and are able to solve them. For well-structured problems, organized matrix-type presentations seem to work the best. More

Figure 3–4. Report from a Member of the Panel of Experts.

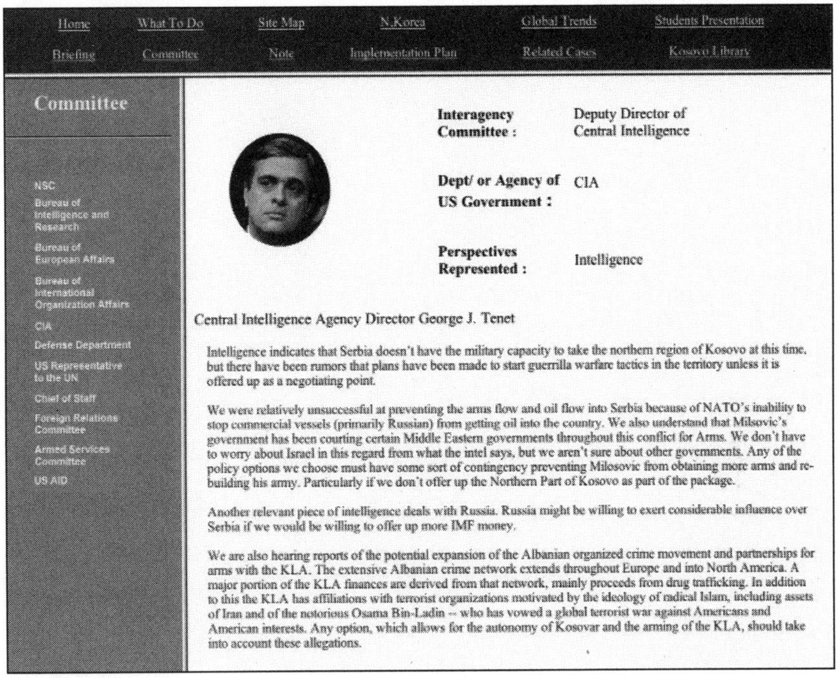

complex and ill-structured problems need to present the underlying complexity and uncertainty of the problem in the problem situation, requiring a less structured representation. And contemporary research consistently shows that situating problems in authentic and meaningful contexts helps learners to understand the problem better and assume more ownership for its solution. More is unknown than known about problem representation, except that it is an important factor in problem solving.

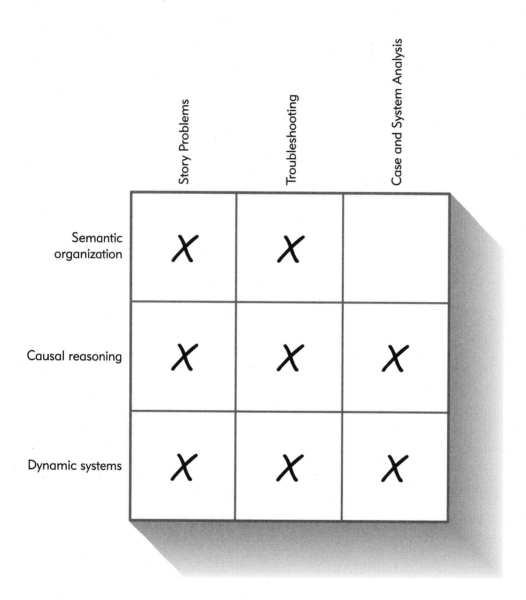

Figure 4–1. Applications of Problem Representation Methods by Problem Type.

4

Tools for Representing Problems by Learners

THE KEY TO PROBLEM solving is how the problem solver represents the problem space, that is, how solvers represent or frame the problem to themselves (Schön, 1979). Simon (1981, p. 153) claimed that "solving a problem simply means representing it so as to make the solution transparent." We know that experts are better problem solvers than novices because they construct richer, more integrated mental representations of problems than do novices (Chi, Feltovich, and Glaser, 1981; Chi and Bassock, 1991; de Jong and Ferguson-Hessler, 1991; Larkin, 1983). Their internal problem representations integrate domain knowledge with the different kinds of problems. That is, experts represent problems in terms of deep-level domain principles, while novices too often represent problems in terms of the surface features of the problem. For example, a story problem in which train A tries to catch up with and overtake train B would be classified by novices as a transportation or travel problem rather than a distance/rate/time problem. Experts, in contrast, represent problems in different ways. Anderson (1983) claims that problems are represented by experts as if-then rules, whereas Chi and

Bassock (1989) and Larkin (1983) showed that experts represent problems in concept mapping forms. Constructing personal problem representations enables problem solvers to guide interpretation of information about the problem, to simulate the behavior of the elements in the problem and properties of the system, and to trigger particular solution processes (Savelsbergh, de Jong, and Ferguson-Hessler, 1998).

Internally representing problems is as important to novice learners as it is to experts. If we want students to be better problem solvers (regardless of problem type), we must teach them to construct problem representations that integrate with domain knowledge. These internal problem representations must be coherent (internally consistent) and should integrate different kinds of representations (qualitative and quantitative, abstract and concrete, visual and verbal).

There are at least two different approaches to helping learners to construct better problem representations, that is, to internally map problems that are presented to them onto their own problem representations. This chapter focuses on how different technology-based tools can be used to help learners externalize their internal problem representations.

The computer-based tools described in this chapter scaffold the ability of learners to represent problems by providing them with tools that qualitatively and sometimes quantitatively model problems. Students who are solving story problems (the most common kind of problem solved in schools) try to directly translate the stated problem into a formula (a quantitative representation). They fail to transfer any problem-solving skill because they make no effort to develop a conceptual, qualitative representation of the problem, which is a necessary prerequisite to representing problems quantitatively (Ploetzner, Fehse, Kneser, and Spada, 1999). That is, students should construct some kind of visual representation of the problem type before attempting to enter values into a formula.

In this chapter, I describe tools that students can use to represent problems qualitatively. Because problems vary, so too should the tools that students use to represent them. For example, Polich and Schwartz (1974) found that matrix representations of problems were especially effective for larger, more complex problems because of the ease of applying and storing the results of logical operations in such a problem space.

It is also likely that individual differences in thinking affect student preferences for representation tool. Jones and Schkade (1995) found that when learners were provided with diagrammatic or table-like tools for representing problems, many of them chose to restructure the problem representations into their preferred mode, diagrams. More research is needed before we fully understand the role of problem representation tools in problem solving.

There are numerous technology tools that learners can use to help them qualitatively represent problem spaces in different ways. One or more of these tools should be used to help learners to build representations of problems that are presented to them. Building representations will help learners to understand and solve problems better.

Representing Semantic Organization

Solving problems first and foremost requires understanding the domain concepts involved in the problem. Unless learners fully understand the meaning of each of the concepts involved in the problem, they will probably not be able to solve it. If they are lucky enough to solve it, they probably will not understand why they were successful or what the solution means.

Meaning for concepts depends on the associations and underlying relationships that each concept has with other concepts. The networks of associations among related concepts are known as *semantic networks*. Semantic networks, also known as *concept maps,* are tools for spatially representing concepts and their interrelationships. Semantic networks represent the knowledge structures (also referred to as *cognitive structures, conceptual knowledge,* and *structural knowledge*) that humans store in their minds (Jonassen, Beissner, and Yacci, 1993). Semantic networking tools graphically represent concepts as nodes and labeled lines representing relationships among them (see Figure 4–2). Semantic networking is the process of constructing these concept maps—of identifying important concepts, arranging those concepts spatially, identifying relationships among those concepts, and labeling the nature of the semantic relationship among those concepts. A detailed description of semantic networking tools and methods is provided by Jonassen (2000b).

Figure 4–2. Semantic Network Describing a Stoichiometry Problem.

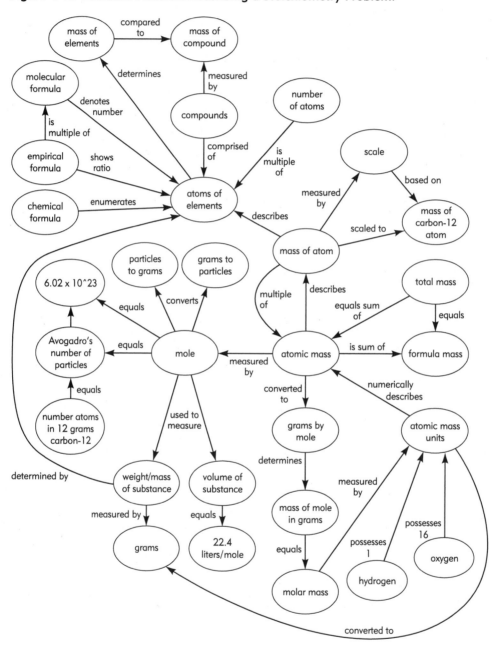

How does semantic networking help problem solving? According to the psychological theory known as schema theory, individual ideas are organized into schemas, and schemas are arranged in networks of interconnected and interrelated ideas known as semantic networks. Understanding any idea therefore depends on how it is related to other ideas in memory. Semantic networking tools are computer-based visualizing tools for representing these semantic networks. Problem solving requires that students understand all of the ideas that are engaged by a problem. Semantic networks help learners to organize what they know about problems by integrating information into a progressively more complex conceptual framework. More important, semantic networks help in increasing the total quantity of formal content knowledge because they facilitate the skill of searching for patterns and relationships among problem components.

Different problems have different structures. Particular problem structures comprise different schemas. That is, different kinds of problems have the same semantic structure. Being able to represent and compare those structures will help learners to classify problems and access appropriate solutions. Building semantic networks as qualitative models of the problem before attempting to solve the problem will help learners understand the components of the problem before they begin solving it. Figure 4–2 illustrates a semantic network of the ideas involved in solving stoichiometry (molar conversion) problems in chemistry. These problems all have a similar semantic structure that defines the relationships among the problem elements.

The semantic network of even a simple molar conversion problem in Figure 4–2 illustrates its underlying complexity. Given that, the importance of creating semantic networks of more complex problems should be obvious. Identifying all of the concepts and themes that connect concepts in a semantic network will help learners to clarify the problem and identify solutions to more ill-structured problems. Semantic networking tools provide valuable assistance in helping learners to represent the meaning and structure of problems that they are solving. If the problems that they are solving have no meaning, they are probably not worth solving. Instructors should always encourage semantic networking before solving problems.

Representing Causal Reasoning

Among the intellectual skills most essential to problem solving are inferencing, predicting, and explaining, all of which are forms of causal reasoning. Causal reasoning usually results from situational conditions, such as an explicit question, an unexpected event, a task failure, or the need to predict some outcome (Hastie, 1984). These cognitive skills all require associating attributes or conditions to outcomes or results. That is, these skills all require an understanding of cause-effect relationships, which is an essential skill in human text comprehension (Schank and Abelson, 1977).

Natural scientific and social scientific systems at all levels are driven by causal events. Human interactions are also compelled by causality. When city drivers exhibit rude behavior, we attribute their behavior to road rage without considering all of the potential causes of that rage (past driving experiences, family relationships, personality type, and so on). Unfortunately, learners usually do not make good use of available information or detecting covariation among problem attributes, they do not detect base rate information, and they confuse opposite conditional probabilities (Nisbett and Ross, 1980). Learners typically use a limited set of oversimplified causal models to explain scientific phenomena (Perkins and Grotzer, 2000). In other words, they are not adept at causal reasoning. Also, causal models needed to explain phenomena are often more complex than those constructed by students. In this section, I describe some mechanisms of causal reasoning and then describe and illustrate a few methods of supporting causal reasoning among learners.

Most of the research and theory development on causal reasoning has emerged from the social psychology literature. This literature focuses on attribution processes. That is, the behavior of a second entity depends on attributes of the first entity. For example, in physics, the distance traveled by an object depends on attributes (velocity and elasticity) of the first object— the sling used to project the object. In other words, the behavior of entities covaries. Humans attribute characteristics to one or more causal agents. One of the best-known theories is Kelly's ANOVA (analysis of variance) model of attribution, where the actors, behaviors, or stimuli covary. "An effect is attributed to one of its possible causes with which, over time, it covaries" (Kelly,

1973, p. 108). When other people respond in the same way (consensus) to similar stimuli (distinctiveness), those attributions are more meaningful.

Another popular conception of causal reasoning is schema based, relating to knowledge structures. That is, individuals construct causal schemas based on their experiences. These schemas are scenario-like and include information about the plans and goals of the actors (Read, 1987), a comprehension process that proceeds somewhat automatically. These scenarios comprise extended sequences of behavior, which have four components: the goal of the sequence, the plan of action, the outcome of the plan, and the conditions that initiated the goal (Read, 1987).

In order to understand causal relations, an individual's causal schemas or scripts must connect the attributions of these components. Actions and events can result in state changes or initiate a mental state, while states can enable or disable actions or events or be reasons for actions (Schank and Abelson, 1977). When schemas are readily available to explain events, causal reasoning is easy. When individuals must construct a schema to explain events (explicit causal reasoning), greater effort is required.

The most useful conception of causal reasoning, I believe, is the mechanistic conception. Mechanism-based causal reasoning refers to explanations of the mediating processes by which the target factors actually produce the effect (Koslowski, Okagaki, Lorenz, and Umbach, 1989). The covariational approach predicts the probability of a cause-effect relationship, and the mechanistic approach explains the underlying semantics of the relationship. Using representations such as influence diagrams or causal maps, mechanistic explanations support qualitative understanding of cause-effect relationships, which enhances understanding. In a recent (and as yet unpublished) study, we found that mechanistic explanations of the causal relationships in physics problems resulted in greater conceptual understanding of the physics principles.

Causal Modeling

Paul Thagard (2000) analyzed the process of diagnosing disease states and concluded that physicians' explanations of diseases, contrary to belief, are not deductive, statistical, or based on single causes. Rather, he described the use of causal networks to depict the combination of inferences needed to reach a diagnosis. These causal networks can be used to model causal reasoning. *Causal modeling* is a generic designation for a group of statistical techniques for describing the causal linkages among correlations. These statistical techniques include LISREL, multiple regression, path analysis, and log-linear analysis. Causal modeling is used when a decision maker or problem solver must deal with trying to "resolve questions about possible causes by providing explanations of phenomena (effects) as the result of previous phenomena (causes)" (Asher, 1983, p. 5). Causal modeling techniques have been used primarily to represent problem solving and decision making in the fields of social science, political science, and physical science due to the cause-and-effect nature of the relationships of the various variables involved in each respective system.

Causal modeling was first used to make medical diagnoses by applying what was called a *deep diagnostic approach* (Console and Torasso, 1990). Jonassen, Mann, and Ambruso (1996) used causal modeling to design a diagnostic learning environment in biomedicine, where physicians first make an initial diagnosis, then determine the etiology, then make a differential diagnosis, followed by treatment and management. Each of these steps entails a different set of causal factors that must be identified. The decisions in this causal sequence are represented in Figure 4–3. The probabilities of the occurrence of each cause can provide feedback to the learner. That is, if the student selects a particular etiology, he is told that based on medical research, there is a certain percentage probability that his selection is correct.

Causal modeling was chosen in order to reflect the uncertainty in the causality of medical diagnostic. At each decision point while working through the case, learners were required to select an initial diagnosis, etiology, or differential diagnosis and support their choice by identifying the causal agents. That is, they were required to justify their decision based on causal reasoning by selecting the probable features that led to their decision.

Causal models constructed by learners or even by designers often are too simple. Adequate causal models tend to be complex. The interactions among factors can be simple linear causality, but are often multiple, interactive, feedback controlled, or constraint based (Perkins and Grotzer, 2000). In ill-structured

Figure 4–3. Causal Model of Medical Diagnosis Used to Structure a Learning Environment.

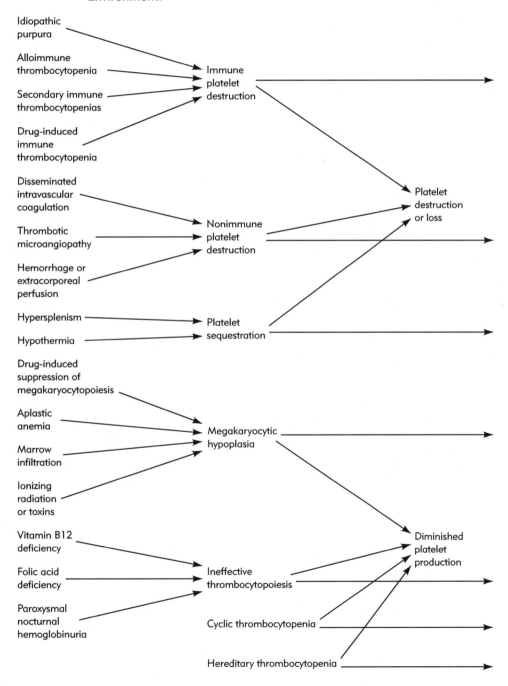

problems, the normally deterministic systems can become chancy, chaotic, or fundamentally uncertain. Learners need to develop a variety of epistemic moves to deal with this underlying complexity, according to Perkins and Grotzer. The methods described below represent some approaches that may help learners construct better causal models.

Influence Diagrams

Another form of causal representation with similar characteristics to semantic networks and causal models is the influence diagram, which is often used as a knowledge acquisition tool for building expert systems (described next). Influence diagrams graphically represent the structure of problems (Moore and Agogino, 1987) as well as depict the interaction of factors that predict an outcome. Influence diagrams represent mechanistic models or causality, as described before. Figure 4–4 describes a story problem–solving learning environment where influence diagrams are used to qualitatively describe the

---

Figure 4–4. Modeling Causal Reasoning with Influence Diagrams in Worked Examples.

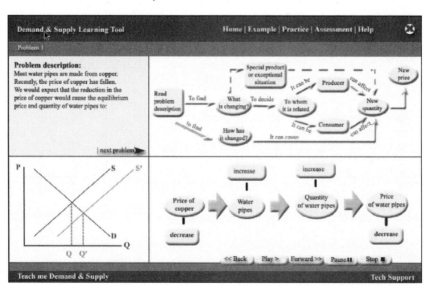

effects of causal influences in determining changes in the supply-and-demand curve. Understanding the effects of shift in the supply-and-demand curves is essential to microeconomics.

Figure 4–5 illustrates an influence diagram of an automotive electrical system to assist in troubleshooting. As indicated in Chapter Two, troubleshooting requires understanding how a system works, especially the functional properties of the system. The mechanic will troubleshoot the problem without resorting to trial and error, serial elimination, or other weak troubleshooting strategies, because she knows how the automotive electrical system works.

We used the systems model in Figure 4–5 as an interface to information about systems components as well as actions to be taken by the troubleshooter. Learners click on the causal factors that they believe are causing the

Figure 4–5. Systems Model for Engine Troubleshooting.

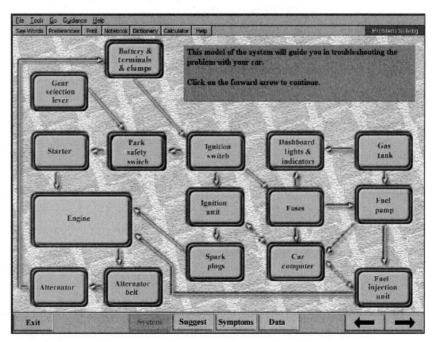

Source: Implemented in the *Problem-Solving Experience* from PLATO Corporation.

problem. Integration or explication of causal factors involved in the problem provides learners with clues about the nature of the problem as well as the conceptual understanding about the nature of the system being troubleshot. They should be included in representations of the problem.

Expert Systems

Another way to represent the causal factors in the problem is to provide an expert system or have the learners construct their own expert system to represent the problem-solving process. Expert systems are artificial intelligence programs designed to simulate the ways that experts think and make decisions. The first major expert system, MYCIN, was developed to help physicians diagnose bacterial infections with which they were unfamiliar. Using conditional if-then logic, expert systems have been developed to help geologists decide where to drill for oil, firefighters decide how to extinguish different kinds of fires, computer sales technicians to configure computer systems, bankers to decide on loan applications, and employees to decide among a large number of company benefits alternatives. Problems whose solutions include recommendations based on a variety of decisions are good candidates for expert systems.

An expert system is a computer program that attempts to simulate the way human experts solve problems—an artificial decision maker. For example, when you consult an expert (a doctor, lawyer, or teacher, for example) about a problem, the expert asks for information about the problem, searches his or her knowledge base (memory) for existing knowledge to relate elements of the current situation to, processes the information (thinks), arrives at a decision, and presents a solution.

Like a human expert, an expert system is approached by an individual with a problem. The system queries the individual about the current status of the problem, searches its knowledge base (which contains previously stored facts and if-then rules), processes the information using its inference engine, arrives at a decision, and reports the solution to the user. The inference engine is the part of an expert system that functions intelligently while querying the knowledge base. It contains the logical programming that examines the information provided by the user, as well as the facts and rules contained within the knowledge base; evaluates the current problem situation; and then seeks out rules that will provide advice about that situation. The expert system is one of the few tools that qualitatively describes causal reasoning. Therefore, it is useful for constructing models of dynamic, causally organized systems.

Using expert systems to model problems is most easily supported using an *expert system shell,* an editor for creating expert systems. Learning how to use most expert system shells can be mastered in less than an hour. When using a shell to construct an expert system rule base, the learner identifies the outcomes or decisions that may be recommended by an expert. Next, the learner identifies the decision factors in the form of questions that will be asked of the user. Writing questions that are simple enough for any novice user to answer is difficult. After identifying the decision factors, the designer writes the rules using if-then logic to relate the decisions to the decision factors or questions. (This process is described more completely by Grabinger, Wilson, and Jonassen, 1990, and Jonassen, 2000b.)

Expert systems have been used to model how students solve simple physics problems, such as battery and bulb combinations (Devi, Tiberghien, Baker, and Brna, 1996). We have constructed expert systems to describe how to solve relatively simple story problems in chemistry. Figure 4–6 lists the decisions, decision factors, and rules for an expert system that simulates the process of solving a story problem in chemistry. Expert systems can provide the most unambiguous descriptions of troubleshooting.

Figure 4–6. Excerpt from an Expert System Rule Base on Solving Stoichiometry Problems.

Context 'This knowledge base is intended to simulate the processes of calculating molar conversions.'

  D1: 'You know the mass of one mole of sample.'
  D2: 'You need to determine molar (formula) mass.'
  D3: 'Divide sample mass by molar mass.'

Figure 4–6. Excerpt from an Expert System Rule Base on Solving Stoichiometry Problems, Cont'd.

D4: 'Multiply number of moles by molar mass.'

D5: 'You know atomic mass units.'

D6: 'You know molar mass.'

D7: 'Divide mass of sample by molar mass and multiply by Avogadro's number.'

D8: 'Divide number of particles by Avogadro's number.'

D9: 'Convert number of particles to moles, then convert moles to mass.'

D10: 'Convert mass to moles using molar mass, and then convert moles to molecules using Avogadro's number.'

D11: 'Convert from volume to moles (divide volume by volume/mole), and then convert moles to moles by multiplying by Avogadro's number.'

Q1: 'Do you know the number of molecules?'   A 1 'yes' 2 'no'

Q2: 'Do you know the mass of the sample in grams?'   A 1 'yes' 2 'no'

Q3: 'Do you know the molar mass of the element or compound?' A 1 'yes' 2 'no'

Q4: 'Do you know the number of moles of the sample?'   A 1 'yes' 2 'no'

Q5: 'Do you want to know the number of molecules?'   A 1 'yes' 2 'no'

Q6: 'Do you want to know the mass of the sample in grams?'   A 1 'yes' 2 'no'

Q7: 'Do you want to know the molar mass of the compound?'   A 1 'yes' 2 'no'

Q8: 'Do you want to know the number of moles of the sample?' A 1 'yes' 2 'no'

Q9: 'Do you know the atomic mass units?'   A 1 'yes' 2 'no'

Q10: 'Do you know the volume of a gas?'   A 1 'yes' 2 'no'

Rule 1: IF q2a1 AND q8a1 THEN D2

Rule 2: IF (d1 OR q3a1) AND q2a1 AND q8a1 THEN D3

Rule 3: IF q4a1 AND q3a1 AND q6a1 THEN D4

Rule 4: IF q3a1 THEN D1

Rule 5: IF q3a1 THEN D5

Rule 6: IF q9a1 THEN D6

Rule 7: IF qq3a1 AND q2a1 AND q5a1 THEN D7

Rule 8: IF q1a1 AND q8a1 THEN D8

Rule 9: IF q1a1 AND q6a1 THEN D9

Rule 10: IF q2a1 AND q5a1 THEN d10

Rule 11: IF q10a1 AND q1a1 THEN d11

Figure 4–7 lists some of the decisions and factors (there are too many rules to display here) for predicting severe weather in a meteorology class. Forecasting weather requires that learners identify the combinations of factors and probabilities that lead to particular predictions. Having students construct these expert systems to represent forecasting thinking helps them to better understand the causal reasoning involved in forecasting and better transfer their forecasting skills. Such expert systems can also be developed as job aids to model troubleshooting processes for learners.

Figure 4–7. Decisions and Factors for an Expert System on Weather Forecasting.

Severe Weather Predictor

This module is designed to assist the severe local storms forecaster in assessing the potential for severe weather using soundings. The program will ask for measures of instability and wind shear, as well as other variables important in the formation of severe weather. Instability and wind shear parameters are easily calculated using programs such as SHARP, RAOB, and GEMPAK. The other variables can be found on surface and upper-air charts.

Advice

The following output indicates the potential for severe weather in the environment represented by the sounding you used. A number between 1 and 10 indicates the confidence of the guidance. A higher number indicates a greater confidence.

Severe Weather (Tornadoes, Hail, and/or Straightline Winds)
Severe Weather Possible
Severe Weather Not Likely
Severe Weather Likely
Severe Weather Potential

Questions (Decision Factors)

What is the value of CAPE (J/kg)? <–6, –2 to –6, 0 to –2, >0
What is the Lifted Index (LI) value (C)? 0, 0-25, 25-75, >75
What is the Convective Inhibition (CIN) (J/kg)? 0, 1-3, >3
What is the Lid Strength Index (LSI) (C)? >450, 250–449, 150–249, 0–150, <150, <0
What is the value of storm-relative helicity? >6, 4–6, 2–4, <2
What is the value of 0–6 km Positive Shear (s-1)?
What is the value of storm-relative helicity (m2 s-1)?
Left Entrance, Right Entrance, Left Exit, Right Exit, None
Which quadrant of the jet streak is the area of interest in? Cold Front, Dryline, Convergence Zone, Outflow Boundary, Nothing Significant
Is there likely to be a significant trigger mechanism? Yes, No

Expert systems can also be used to model belief systems or options for solving complex case problems as well as simpler story and troubleshooting problems. Figure 4–8 lists an expert system rule base that models the reasoning that one student believed that President Truman used in deciding whether to drop the atomic bomb on Hiroshima. This is one student's speculation. Many different beliefs and reasoning patterns could also be modeled and tested using expert systems. What makes expert systems and systems models (described next) so powerful is that the effects of various conditions can be tested and revised in order to simulate problem-solving activities like decision making.

Figure 4–8. Expert System Rule Base for the Hiroshima Scenario.

Decision 1: 'Atomic fission should only be used for peaceful purposes.'

Decision 2: 'The atomic bomb should be used as quickly as possible primarily on military targets.'

Decision 3: 'Only knowledge of the weapons existence should be used as a threat to induce Japan to surrender.'

Decision 4: 'The atomic bomb should not be used, but research should be made known after war ends.'

Question 1: 'Do you want to encourage the Japanese to surrender as quickly as possible?'

Answers   1 'Yes.'

               2 'No.'

Question 2: 'Do you want to limit the loss of Allied and Japanese lives?'

Answers   1 'Yes.'

               2 'No.'

Question 3: 'Do you want to use the weapon against the Germans?'

Answers   1 'Yes.'

               2 'No.'

               3 'Unsure.'

Figure 4–8. Expert System Rule Base for the Hiroshima Scenario, Cont'd.

Question 4: 'Do you want to use the atomic fission research ONLY to create alternate sources of energy?'

Answers   1 'Yes.'

              2 'No.'

              3 'Unsure.'

Question 5: 'Do you want to increase the political power of the Allies during and after the war?'

Answers   1 'Yes.'

              2 'No.'

              3 'Unsure.'

Question 6: 'Do you believe the Japanese will surrender with continued conventional bombing of Japanese cities?'

Answers   1 'Yes.'

              2 'No.'

              3 'Unsure.'

Question 7: 'Was the Manhattan Project (development of atomic fission) initially begun primarily for future military use?'

Answers   1 'Yes.'

              2 'No.'

              3 'Unsure.'

Question 8: 'Do you want to end the Japanese march through Asia?'

Answers   1 'Yes.'

              2 'No.'

              3 'Unsure.'

Question 9: 'Do you want to use atomic fission as only a psychological weapon?'

Answers   1 'Yes.'

              2 'No.'

              3 'Unsure.'

Question 10: 'How much longer should the war continue (from Spring 1945)?'

Answers   1 '3 months.'

              2 '6 months.'

              3 '1 year.'

              4 'Indefinitely.'

Figure 4–8. Expert System Rule Base for the Hiroshima Scenario, Cont'd.

Rule 1:   IF Question 1=Answer 1 & Question 2=Answer 1 & Question 5=Answer 1
THEN Decision 2 .

Rule 2:   IF Question 3=Answer 2 THEN Decision 4.

Rule 3:   IF Question 4=Answer 1 THEN Decision 3.

Rule 4:   IF Question 4=Answer 2 THEN Decision 2.

Rule 5:   IF Question 5=Answer 1 & Question 6=Answer 2 THEN Decision 2.

Rule 6:   IF Question 6=Answer 1 THEN Decision 4.

Rule 7:   IF Question 6=Answer 2 & Question 1=Answer 1 & Question 8=Answer 1
THEN Decision 2.

Rule 8:   IF Question 6=Answer 3 THEN Decision 3.

Rule 9:   IF Question 7=Answer 1 & Question 1=Answer 1 THEN Decision 2.

Rule 10: IF Question 7=Answer 2 THEN Decision 1.

Rule 11: IF Question 7=Answer 3 THEN Decision 4.

Rule 12: IF Question 8=Answer 1 & Question 6=Answer 2 & Question 1=Answer 1
THEN Decision 2.

Rule 13: IF Question 8=Answer 2 THEN Decision 3.

Rule 14: IF Question 9=Answer 1 THEN Decision 3.

Rule 15: IF Question 9=Answer 2 & Question 8=Answer 1 & Question 7=Answer 1
& Question 1=Answer 1 THEN Decision 2.

Rule 16: IF Question 4=Answer 1 & Question 5=Answer 1 & Question 7=Answer 3
THEN Decision 4.

Rule 17: IF Question 10=Answer 1 & Question 2=Answer 1 & Question 6=Answer 3
THEN Decision 2.

Rule 18: IF Question 10=Answer 2 & Question 3=Answer 1 & Question 5=Answer 1
THEN Decision 2.

Rule 19: IF Question 10=Answer 3 & Question 6=Answer 1 & Question 8=Answer 3
THEN Decision 4.

Rule 20: IF Question 10=Answer 4 & Question 4=Answer 1 & Question 6=Answer 3
THEN Decision 4.

A note of caution is in order. Attribution theory, on which causality is based, describes the antecedent conditions to which the effect is associated. The information about attributions in particular events is represented by the learner in a mental model based on simple rules of inference from which the learner can explain phenomena (Jaspers, 1988). It is important to note that not all conditional statements are causal. "If today is June 21, then tomorrow is June 22" is not causal. Such statements are correlational (conditions covary), but the condition does not cause an effect. For instance, the number of fast-food hamburgers sold is correlated with the rate of obesity in America. However, hamburgers sold did not cause obesity, which is attributable to hamburgers (and other high-fat foods) consumed, a lack of exercise, genetic dispositions, and so on. Problem solving often requires accommodating a combination of causal and noncausal conditions. It is also important for learners to recognize which conditions are necessary and which are sufficient.

Modeling Dynamic Systems

Ill-structured problems are difficult to solve because the behavior of the system in which the problem occurs is not predictable. Thus, solving ill-structured problems often requires a different perspective: a systems perspective. There are two important ideas in systems theory that need to be represented by learners in order to solve many ill-structured problems.

First, causality is too often conceived by students as a one-way process. Hunger causes eating. Although that is partially true, what causes the cessation of eating, or does the organism continue eating until it bursts? Most systems in which problems occur can also be seen as closed-loop systems, in which the components of those systems are interdependent and controlled by feedback. The perception of hunger causes eating, which occurs until the perception ceases (feedback), which causes a cessation of the eating behavior until the perception occurs again (another form of feedback). Something that is initially an effect can become a cause.

Second, most real-world systems are dynamic; they change over time. In well-structured problems, the entities do not change, but in everyday problems, the entities in the problem are constantly changing. They may be affected by each other or by external forces. Hunger states, for example, change not only with the volume of eating but also may depend on the levels of exercise or the kinds of food available.

A popular method for representing dynamic problems is the use of causal loop diagrams, which show the causal relationships and circular feedback in systems (see Figure 4–9). They illustrate the interdependence of system parts, specifically the conditions under which system components are interdependent and the effects of that interdependence. Figure 4–9 describes the causal relationships in a family where a husband who is stressed at work fights more with his wife, which in turn causes more stress. Fighting causes a reduction in the strength of their relationship, and as the relationship crumbles, stress increases, which causes more fighting, and so on. In order to build causal loop diagrams, students must determine the choices that are available in a system and the trade-offs that result from those choices. Articulating the various causes that affect a problem is necessary to being able to solve it.

Figure 4–9. Causal Loop Diagram of a Family Problem.

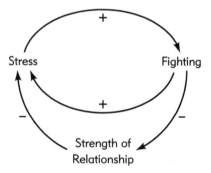

Causal loop diagrams can depict the interdependencies of systems, but they cannot be tested. In order to do that, problems must be represented by systems modeling tools, such as Stella, Ven Sim, or PowerSim. These tools provide editors for visually representing the interdependent parts of a system, analyzing and quantifying the cumulative effects of relationships of parts on each other, and testing the model of the system. Developing a model of a system operationalizes the system, allowing the problem solver to try out different systems options and make decisions based on the performance of the system. Figure 4–10 illustrates a systems model and its output for a story problem in chemistry. This is a well-structured story problem with few inputs and fairly reliable outputs.

Figure 4–10. Systems Dynamics Model of a Stoichiometry Problem in Stella.

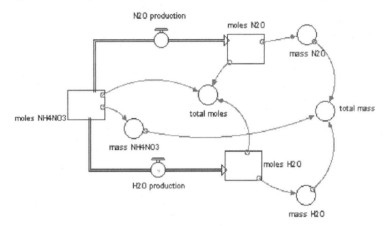

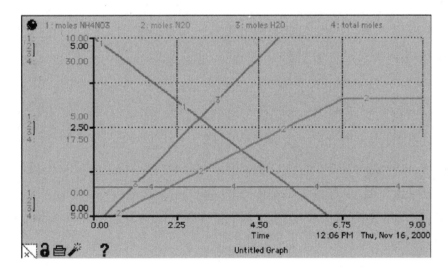

Learning to troubleshoot can also benefit from constructing systems models. So can learning about troubleshooting. In Figure 4–11, we constructed a model of the troubleshooting process. This is a cognitive simulation of a thinking process that helped us to develop our understanding of the troubleshooting process.

Figure 4–11. Systems Model of a Troubleshooting Process.

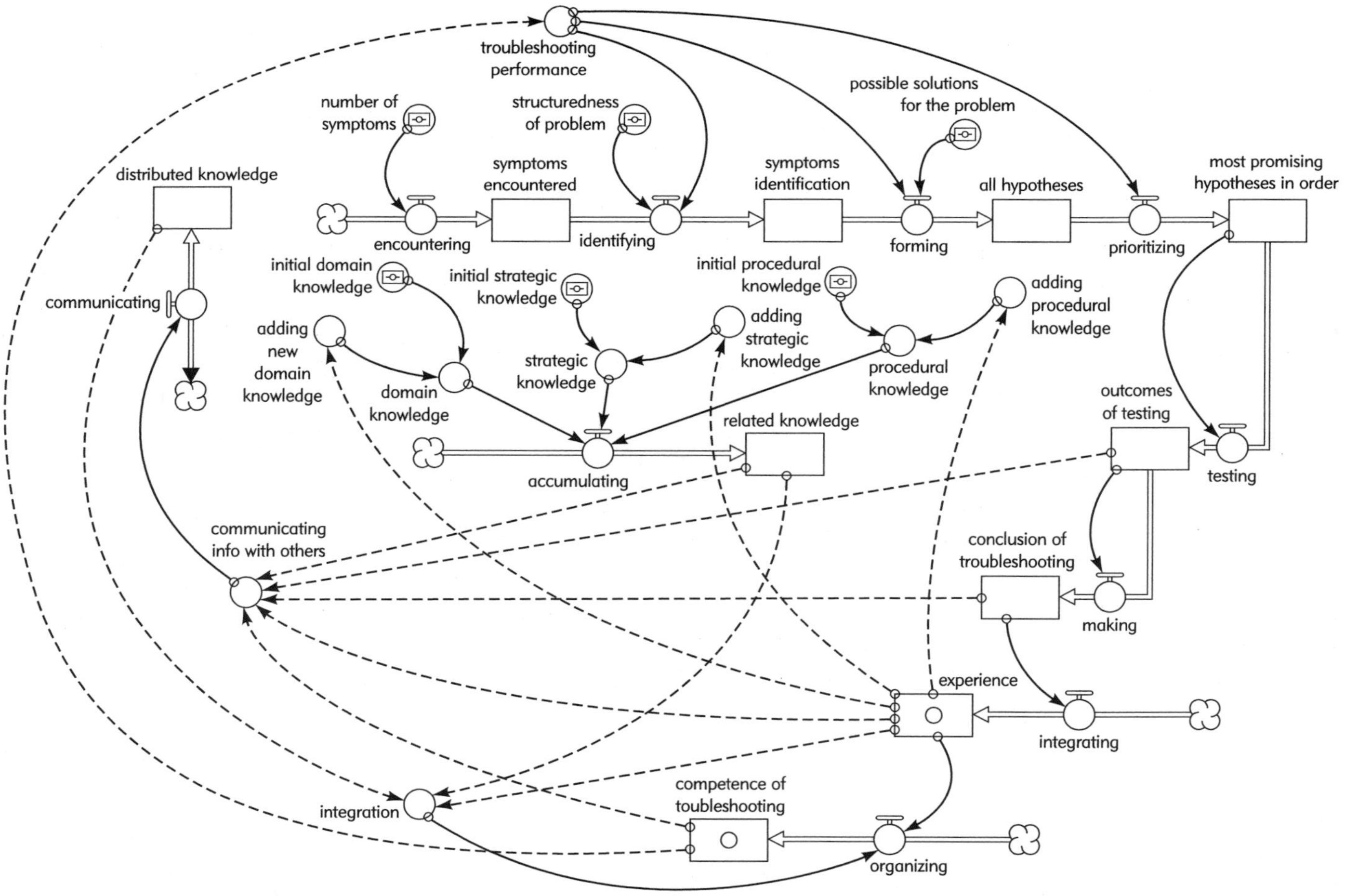

When solving more complex problems, such as resolving the Arab-Israeli conflict, the social, religious, economic, and political systems are much more complex, and so the models of the systems must be more complex. Figure 4–12 shows the beginning of a systems model that attempts to identify the important dynamic relationships in that conflict. This model would support a case analysis problem that called on learners to find a solution. What makes systems models so powerful is that the builder can run the simulation that is defined by the model and dynamically redefine the variables until the result models either reality or the desired behavior.

Figure 4–12. Systems Model of the Arab-Israeli Conflict.

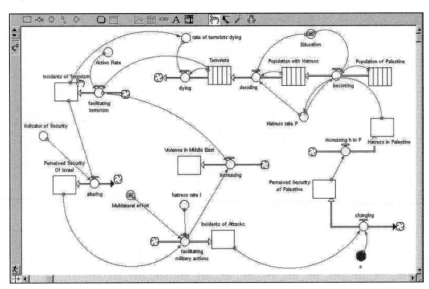

SUMMARY

The key to successful problem solving, many believe, is the mental construction of the problem space. When presented with a problem, the problem solver must reconcile what kind of problem it is; what its factors or components and parameters are; how they interact; and so on.

In this chapter, I have demonstrated three methods for externalizing those problem spaces. Using semantic or causal representations, like influence diagrams, expert systems, or systems models, designers or teachers can present models as simulations for students to test; better yet, students can construct models of the problem they are trying to solve. The better that we understand a problem, the more likely it will be that we can solve it. In the previous chapter, I described how teachers can represent problems to learners. In this chapter, I have focused on how learners can represent problems for themselves.

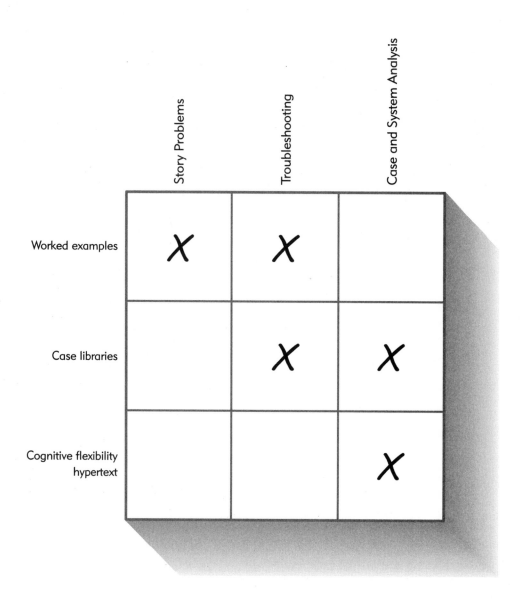

Figure 5–1. Application of Methods to Problem Types.

5

Associating Solutions with Problems

ONCE THEY HAVE developed an understanding of the problem, problem solvers must begin the search for solutions to it. Different types of problems require different ways of generating and associating solutions with different problems. The focus of this chapter is how to teach learners to solve problems once they have adequately represented them.

When most people are asked to teach something to someone else, they almost invariably default to procedural demonstration. "First, you do this. Then you do this," and so on. The limitation of that approach is that when we learn only the procedure for accomplishing the task, we do not construct any conceptual understanding of the system in which the problem occurs, the strategic knowledge about when and why to follow the procedure, and many other intellectual perspectives on the task. Procedures may be adequate for solving simple, well-structured problems, but if the procedure fails to work, learners are lost. Experts are expert because they know about their domain in different ways, not just one. This is especially true in problem solving. If a problem solver understands how to solve a problem in only one way (for example, through a procedure), then he or she will not be able to transfer problem-solving skills successfully. If a step in the procedure is left out or produces an unexpected result or if attributes of the problem change, the problem solver will be at a loss to know how to proceed.

It is impossible to adequately "teach" learners how to solve problems by conveying a procedure because procedures are not foolproof. No one can "teach" ill-structured problems using a procedural approach, because there usually is no procedure to be applied. In this chapter, I describe three methods for "teaching" problem solving: worked examples, case libraries, and cognitive flexibility hypertexts.

Worked Examples: Modeling Performance

In order to understand worked examples, it is necessary to understand a little bit about human cognition. Problem solving is hard work because it places cognitive demands on the learner.

When faced with a problem, learners usually attempt to retrieve everything that they know about solving that kind of problem. Whatever knowledge they retrieve is transferred, according to information processing models of cognition, into working memory, a temporary memory buffer that holds information for short periods of time. The capacity of working memory is limited—usually to two or three items that are being manipulated, compared, or otherwise processed (Sweller, van Merrienboer, and Paas, 1998). So when learners retrieve what they know about solving a problem plus having to juggle elements of the current problem they are trying to solve, working memory can easily become overloaded. Information about the problem or the solution procedures falls out and has to be reaccessed, bumping something else out of working memory. Demands on working memory make problem solving more difficult.

One way to reduce demand on working memory is to retrieve better-organized and more integrated memories about the problem being solved. A common conception of those memories is the *schema,* which is a cognitive representation of a construct (an idea, concept, process, or phenomenon, for example). A schema for some phenomenon consists of all of the attributes that are associated with that idea. Say a word, and then think as quickly as possible of the first ten things that come to your mind when you say that word. Those associations form a rough model of a schema. A schema for a problem consists of the kind of problem it is, the structural elements of the problem (such as acceleration, distance, and velocity in a physics problem), situations in which such problems occur (inclined planes and automobiles, for example), and the processing operations required to solve that problem (Jonassen, 2003). When schemas are well organized and integrated, they can be brought into working memory as a whole chunk, thereby placing lower demands on working memory. The development of problem schemas can be supported by explicitly modeling the structure of the problem during the worked example (Jonassen, 2003) and by practicing solving particular kinds of problems. With extensive practice and reflection, schemas for different kinds of problems become automated. This is how experts become such good problem solvers. When they see a problem, they immediately classify its type and execute their schema, which includes conceptual knowledge, processing operations, and fix-up strategies. Rather than having to perform numerous steps in analyzing and setting up the problem, the expert fires a schema that contains necessary knowledge or operations.

A body of research that has examined how to teach problem solving by reducing cognitive load and supporting problem schema development has focused on worked examples. Conventional approaches to problem-solving instruction present basic principles, usually in an abstract way, followed by extensive practice on problems: "Here is a rule or principle about the world. Now see if you can apply that rule to solving a problem." Sweller and Cooper (1985) investigated an alternative approach to teaching problem solving in algebra that provides worked-out examples of problem solutions to learners. In this approach, learners acquire an understanding of the basic principles of algebra and study a series of worked-out examples: instructional devices that typically include the problem statement and a procedure for solving the prob-lem (Exhibit 5–1) for the purpose of showing how other problems may be

---

Exhibit 5–1. Worked Example of a Simple Problem.

PROBLEM: A car is driving from Kansas City to St. Louis, a distance of 250 miles. At 50 miles per hour, how long will it take to travel between the two cities?

SOLUTION
Step 1:
Total distance between cities: 250 miles
Rate (velocity) of travel: 50 miles per hour

Step 2:
If distance = rate × time
Then time = distance/rate

Step 3:
Distance of 250 miles divided by 50 miles per hour equals 5 hours.

ANSWER: The time required to drive from Kansas City to St. Louis is 5 hours.

---

solved (Atkinson, Derry, Renkl, and Wortham, 2000). Sweller and Cooper found that the worked-example approach was significantly less time-consuming than the conventional problem-solving method. Furthermore, learners required significantly less time to solve similar problems and made significantly fewer errors than did their counterparts. They concluded that the use of worked examples may redirect attention away from the problem goal and toward problem-state configurations and their associated moves.

The traditional approach to solving problems is means-ends: students identify the goal and work backward to figure out what needs to be done next. This approach imposes a heavier cognitive load on working memory because learners have to pay attention to differences in problem states rather than to each state and its associated moves. Worked examples reduce that cognitive load and improve performance unless the worked examples require learners to integrate multiple sources of information mentally (Sweller, 1989; Ward and Sweller, 1990).

Subgoals

Another issue that has been researched relative to worked examples is the explication of subgoals in the problem. Rather than remembering a set of steps for solving problems, Catrambone (1994, 1996) claims that it is important that worked examples explicitly describe the subgoals that are important to the knowledge domain embedded in the steps. When individual steps in a problem solution may change but the overall procedure remains the same, students often fail to transfer their skills when they are not aware of the subgoals required to solve the problem. In series of experiments, Catrambone showed that students who studied solutions emphasizing subgoals were more likely to solve new problems requiring subgoals.

Self-Explanations

A newer issue that has been investigated relative to worked examples is the role of self-explanations. Mwangi and Sweller (1998) asked third graders to self-reflect by asking them "to pretend they were explaining the solution to another child who did not know how to solve the problem" (p. 180). Otherwise known as a *teachback* (described more fully in Chapter Seven), this method is intended to support schema development by having problem solvers reflect on what they have done and attempt to integrate it with what they already know. Although Mwangi and Sweller found no benefit from self-explanations, Renkl, Stark, Gruber, and Mandl (1998) found that self-explanations improved the ability to transfer problem-solving skills to similar and dissimilar problems. Understandably, the quality of the self-explanation best predicted the ability to transfer. Self-explanations occur naturally among learners. Chi and others (1989) found that higher-achieving students naturally generate self-explanations by expanding their solutions to other problems and monitoring their own understanding and misunderstanding. Those self-explanations come from knowledge acquired while trying to instantiate ideas while reading the text and also from generalizing those example statements (Chi and VanLehn, 1991). Self-explanations require active and intentional attempts to make sense out of what is being studied.

In an extensive review of the research on worked examples, Atkinson, Derry, Renkl, and Wortham (2000) provide a number of recommendations about how to use and present worked examples:

- For each type of problem being learned, multiple worked examples should be used.

- For each type of problem being learned, multiple forms (situations) should be used.

- Examples of each kind of problem should be paired.

- For each example, present the worked example using different modalities (for example, aural, visual).

- For each example, clarify the subgoal structure of the problem.

- Encourage the use of self-explanations during and after solution.

Using Worked Examples

Although a great deal has been learned about using worked examples, a great deal more has yet to be learned. One of the more important issues for this book relates to the kinds of problems for which worked examples may be effective. Virtually all of the research on worked examples has been conducted using story problems, so we have no idea how well they may work with other kinds of problems. As indicated in Figure 5–1 (see page 84), worked examples are appropriate for story problems and certain aspects of troubleshooting problems. However, they will likely be of no value for case analysis problems. I say *likely* because we do not know. No one has ever researched the use of worked examples with ill-structured problems.

The following brief description sets out how I believe that worked examples should be used in a computer-based learning environment for teaching students how to solve kinematics problems in physics. In this environment, an animated agent (let's call him Einstein) will appear on the screen over the problem. Einstein first reads the verbal problem representation in the upper-right-hand corner of the screen shown in Figure 5–2, looking for clues to help to classify the problem type (in our example, constant). The agent then selects that problem type and reflects on why that was an appropriate choice (modeling self-explanation). It is not clear whether self-explanations are better modeled during problem solution or after.

Figure 5–2. Screen 1 of a Learning Environment Using a Worked Example.

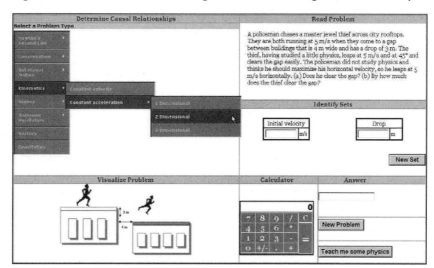

Having classified and justified the problem as a two-dimensional constant acceleration problem in Figure 5–2, the screen in Figure 5–3 appears. Einstein next plans the solution by explicitly identifying the required subproblems. The subproblems are added to the Plan Solution box as they are being performed— for example, (1) choose the point of origin, (2) choose the system of reference (*x*-axis and *y*-axis), (3) determine the time in air (initial velocity plus how much it moved on the *y*-axis), or (4) determine the range of projectile motion on the *x*-axis. Einstein uses the Set Identifier in Figure 5–3 to identify the sets from the problem statement that are required for the problem, justifying why each is important as he moves them into the set identifier. Next, Einstein moves those sets onto the structural model in Figure 5–3 (Determine Causal Relationships). The structural model is a domain-specific model of the problem, showing the relationships of problem components to each other. This step is intended to help learners construct principled problem schemas rather than those based on surface-level characteristics. Einstein then maps the values in the structural model onto the formula in the equation builder, again explaining why those structural elements are represented the way they are in the formula. Einstein next performs a unit check and estimates the size of the answer.

Figure 5–3. Screen 2 of a Learning Environment Using a Worked Example.

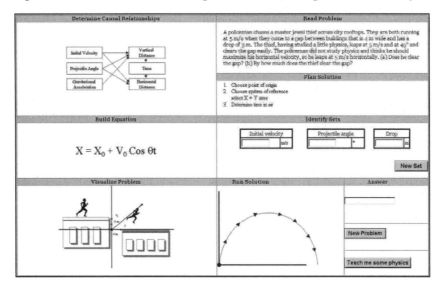

He then solves the formula and reconciles the outcome with the estimate and the vector map shown under Run Solution. Performing this demonstration with two other more complex problems prepares the student for completing practice items.

Many of the elements of this environment go beyond the research findings on worked examples to date. Obviously, empirical validation of the model is required before we know which are the essential processes.

Case Libraries: Teaching with Stories

In formal education (K-12, universities, and corporate training), almost all instruction is "about" a topic. In high school, we learn about geography. In college, we learn about sociology, and in corporate training, we learn about management. The goal of most instruction is the transmission of content—content that is arranged hierarchically in tables of content. The major problem with this approach is that this organization is opposed to the way that humans naturally think. Throughout history, the dominant method for communicating and conveying ideas has been to tell stories. Stories can be used very effectively as instructional support systems helping people learn to solve problems.

Humans appear to have an innate ability and predisposition to organize and represent their experiences in the form of stories. Stories require less cognitive effort to frame experience in the narrative form (Bruner, 1990). Being part of a culture is being connected to the stories of that culture (Bruner, 1990). Stories help us to negotiate meaning, learn about the past, understand human actions and intentions, create an identity, and understand our experiences in the world.

Given their importance to understanding ourselves and the world around us, why are stories not a commonly accepted form of teaching and learning along with logical exposition? Stories traditionally have represented a scientifically unacceptable form of logic. They have been considered entertainment (McEwan and Egan, 1995, p. xii) and so were not seriously viewed as an alternative form of explanation in most disciplines, except for history, anthropology, and qualitative sociology. Logical exposition, the preferred medium for scientific discourse, applies formal and empirical proofs, while narrative convinces through verisimilitude (Bruner, 1990). Logical exposition has traditionally been used to teach problem solving, because education was impelled to appear scientific in its discourse. Despite the dominance of logical forms of exposition in academic disciplines, it is the narrative form of explanation that "just plain folks" (Lave, 1988) use in their everyday negotiations of meaning and problem solving. Narrative seems to convey its message in an inherently human dimension, a dimension that is inexorably lost in a logical exposition (McEwan and Egan, 1995; Polkinghorne, 1988).

Despite their historical lack of status for solving problems in the workplace, stories are almost always used in the process. Polkinghorne (1988) found that practitioners primarily prefer to work with narrative knowledge when asked to provide explanations. "They work with case histories and use narrative explanations to understand why the people they work with behave the way they do" (p. x). Schön (1993) studied architects, engineers, and psychotherapists and found that they most often encoded their experiences in narrative form by using case histories and narrative explanations. In an ethnographic study of problem solving among refrigeration service technicians, Henning (1996) found that stories served as a mechanism for promoting an ongoing discourse between technician, machines, products, and people. By telling stories to their coworkers, technicians were able to build their community of practice. Orr (1996) found that diagnosis happens through stories for framing and dealing with problems. Narrative was used for explaining catastrophes; for understanding, explaining, and arriving at diagnoses; for teaching and learning new methods; for dealing with uncertainty; for changing perspectives on problems; for warning about failures; for providing solutions; for expanding the problem space; for finding causes to problems; for illustrating a point; for challenging a fellow technician; for building confidence as problem solvers; and for anticipating future problems. Many other researchers have shown that narrative is a primary medium for problem solving.

If stories are so essential to learning to solve problems in everyday and professional contexts, we should also consider their use in education and training, especially for ill-structured problems that do not have single solutions, are open-ended, are composed of many subproblems, frequently have many possible solution paths, and possess no clear beginning or end (Jonassen, 1997; Kolodner, Hmelo, and Narayanan, 1996; Sinnott, 1989). Klein and Calderwood (1988) found that experts (fire commanders, tank commanders, and system designers) relied more heavily on cases based on past experience than on abstract principles when making decisions with a high degree of uncertainty. Perhaps the use of previous cases is nowhere more obvious than with automobile mechanics, who use their experiences and those of others when wrestling with new problems (Lancaster and Kolodner, 1988). And Kopeikina, Brandau, and Lemmon (1988) found similar evidence with GTE engineers who were troubleshooting phone switching networks. The reuse of cases is essential to learning how to perform complex tasks.

How can stories be used to teach problem solving? Given the lack of previous experiences among novices, experiences available through a case library augment their repertoire of experiences. These prior experiences help novices to interpret current and future stories, forewarn them of potential problems, realize what to avoid, and foresee the consequences of their decisions or actions.

Supporting Problem Solving with Stories

Teaching with cases presumes that students encounter a problem to solve and then try to construct a representation of the problem. If students encounter difficulties in constructing a representation of the problem or generating a hypothesis or solution, we can provide access to cases previously solved by an experienced problem solver and related through a story. Why? When confronted with a problem, people first try to remember a case in which they faced a similar situation (Schank, 1990, 1999). If they identify a similar case, they reuse the solution to solve the current problem. If the current problem is similar, they will attempt to adapt the solution to the prior experience to the new situation. If the solution works, they will reindex the adapted case and remember it as a new story that may be applicable to another situation.

There are different ways that case libraries can be used to support learning to solve problems. First, stories can be made available in a structured (indexed) form, so when students run into difficulties, they can access the case library and search for a story based on similar symptoms and circumstances, selected by students based on their perceived relevance. An example of a case library that may be accessed and searched is a turfgrass management library (see Figure 5–4).

Figure 5–4. Case Library of Turfgrass Problems.

Welcome to the Turfgrass Management Case Library. These stories were gathered to help students and professionals learn about real-world problems encountered in turf management and the solutions used to solve those problems. The stories have been provided by members of the USGA Greens Section and represent actual problems encountered in the field.

To access the stories make a selection from the pull-down menus below. The first set of menus represent the turf species at the problem area. The second set of menus represent the turf type (for example, a golf course green). The third set of menus represent the problem that was encountered.

After you have made your selections click on the "Access the Case Library" button and you will be given a list of cases that correspond to the choices you have made.

Choose one or two turf species:
| all cool-season grasses | ⬍ | buffalograss | ⬍ |

Choose one or two turf types:
| golf course, general | ⬍ | fairway | ⬍ |

Choose one or two problems you would like to look at:
| compaction | ⬍ | mowing damage | ⬍ |

Golf course managers or students who are learning about golf course management and are looking for help in solving a turfgrass problem such as drainage, bare spots, or excessive weeds may log onto the Web site and select cases based on specific grass species, the purpose of the turf, or the nature of potential problems in order to compare these teaching cases with the problem cases they are working on. The case tells a story of the problem, what the manager did to solve the problem and why, and how successful the solution was. The most important index in most cases (stories) is the lessons learned. The student may choose to try the solution proffered, adapt it to meet local needs, or reject the advice provided by the case. Students learn that there is no single correct solution to most applied problems. There are usually several solutions, some of which are more effective than others. Using cases in this way convinces the student of the uncertainty in solving complex and ill-structured problems.

The Knowledge Innovation for Technology in Education (KITE) project is building a case library of technology integration stories told by teachers about their experiences in attempting to integrate technology into their classrooms (Wang, Jonassen, Strobel, and Cernusca, forthcoming). The project has collected hundreds of stories from teachers about their successes and their failures in integrating technology in their classrooms.

It is important for case libraries to represent failures as well as successes, because we tend to learn more from our failures. When designing lessons and thinking about integrating technologies into those lessons, new or experienced teachers may use the interface shown in Figure 5–5 to access stories about other experiences to provide advice about what works or what may not work. Based on the indexes that teachers choose to search, the program uses an algorithm to access the cases that are most relevant to the teacher's query. The teacher uses that advice in designing lessons.

Case libraries such as KITE and the turfgrass library can be used in different ways. They can function as electronic performance support systems accessible to practitioners or others seeking advice on problems. And they can be used as support systems in problem-based learning environments for novices learning about a new field, the application described next.

Figure 5–5. Access to the Case Library on Technology Integration Stories.

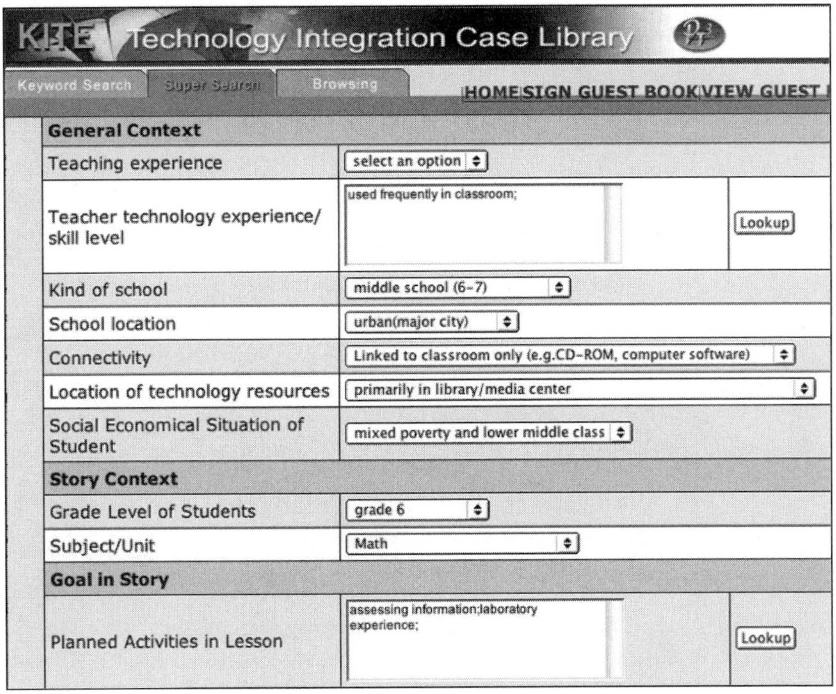

Another way that stories may be used during learning is to construct a program that automatically selects a case and presents it to the students when they experience problems. Figure 5–6 is a screen from a complex food product development problem developed for an agricultural economics course. Specific learning issues are raised about the case at key points in the text—for example, the issue of ascertaining potential market size. To the right of this learning issue is an icon alluding to a story and its main theme. When the mouse slides over it, a pop-up flashes the story's title that corresponds to an "index" (Schank, 1999) to that story.

Stories were collected by presenting three food product developer practitioners with the "Market Potential" section of the case being solved by the

Figure 5–6. Food Product Development Problem.

students. For each learning issue, each practitioner was asked if the issues being presented brought to mind a professional problem that he or she had experienced. The phrase "Let me tell you a story . . ." appears on the browser's status line at the same time to alert students to the availability of a story. Clicking on it accessed the story shown in Exhibit 5–2.

There were twenty-four stories corresponding to different learning issues available to students as they worked through the problem. Hernandez-Serrano and Jonassen (2003) showed that on tests assessing problem-solving skills, such as reminding, identifying and recognizing the problem, identifying and explaining failure, selecting solutions, adapting solutions, explaining success or alternate

---

Exhibit 5–2. Story Told to Students Solving the Food Product Development Problem.

Understanding Market Strength, Market Share and Market Size

Coca-Cola's Share of the Stomach

In 1980, less than 15% of Coca-Cola's sales came from outside the U.S. Having been a dominant player in the U.S. for so long, the company was having a hard time finding opportunities for growth despite its enormous market strength. Coca-Cola's CEO, Roberto Crispulo Goizueta, challenged its employees to make the company a dominant player all over the world. Without changing the product, he drove Coca-Cola's marketing machine to push the product nationally and internationally by simply modifying Coca-Cola's definition of market strength, which up to that moment was defined as the company's share of the cola market.

His strategy was very simple. He called it "the share of the stomach." That is, if any person around the world drank liquids 20–25 times a day, Coca-Cola's target was that one of those drinks be a Coke. Mr. Goizueta's insight was that Coca-Cola was in the business of selling liquids and it had to compete with coffee, water, juice or any other liquid consumed by an average person around the world. He changed the thought process of the entire organization from the perception that the company was a dominant player in the cola market to a company that was measuring its potential market size by focusing on Coke's share of the stomach. This prompted Coca-Cola executives to venture into the business of juice, water and other liquids in order to increase Coca-Cola's share of the stomach.

In 1982, 80% of Coca-Cola's sales came from the U.S. and 20% from overseas. By 1997, Coca-Cola's sales were 20% from the U.S.—while still holding the dominant market position—and 80% from overseas. This had been one of the most successful growth strategies in recent times. Coca-Cola's success made many executives in other businesses rethink their definitions for market strength, market share and market size.

---

strategies, and identifying needed information, students who received stories outperformed students who received expository help in lieu of the stories.

Students may also have access to a case library that will automatically access stories based on their performance. When a student makes a seemingly incorrect response or chooses an inappropriate action, for example, the learning environment will select a case that tells a story relevant to the response.

The case may reinforce the student action, provide an alternative solution, or correct the student's response. The best-known model for this type of case-based teaching is the goal-based scenario (GBS). In GBSs, students become active participants in complex systems. They employ a "learning by doing" architecture (Schank, Fano, Bell, and Jona, 1993/94) in which they are immersed in a focused, goal-oriented situation and required to perform authentic, real-world activities. They are supported with advice in the form of stories that are indexed and accessed using an access algorithm. This automatic case-based reasoning analysis identifies instructive cases that teach a lesson to the learner.

Collecting Stories

In order to build case libraries to support problem solving, it is first necessary to elicit and capture relevant stories about previously solved problems from the practitioners. The goal of capturing stories is to collect a set of stories that can provide lessons to the problem solver that will help solve the problem. Jonassen and Hernandez-Serrano (2002) described a method for collecting stories from practitioners:

1. Identify skilled practitioners who have solved problems similar to the ones that are being presented to the students. Skilled practitioners are those who have some years of experience in solving problems similar to the ones being analyzed.

2. Show the practitioners the problems, one problem at a time. Ask the practitioners if they can remember any similar problems that they have solved. If they can, allow them to tell a story about the problem without interruption.

3. Following the telling of the story, analyze it with the practitioner. Work with the practitioner to identify the problem goals, the context in which the problem occurred, the solution that was chosen and why, and the outcome of the solution. It is important to identify the points that each story makes, that is, the lessons that it can teach.

Following story telling, the cases should probably be indexed, a process that is set out in Kolodner (1993).

Cognitive Flexibility Hypertexts: Conveying Complexity

The ability to solve very complex and ill-structured problems requires that students learn to think differently than they normally do in classrooms and training sessions, where they focus on memorization and comprehension. Students are unable to solve ill-structured problems because they cannot think flexibly enough. Throughout their education, they are taught only one point of view: that of their teachers. If students comprehend that point of view well enough to pass the quiz or exam, they are rewarded with a good grade.

These approaches to instruction, however, contribute to errors in conceptual understanding (Feltovich, Spiro, and Coulson, 1989). Learning only one perspective oversimplifies any idea in any field of study, especially when we attempt to apply the ideas in that field (Coulson, Feltovich, and Spiro, 1989). Why do teachers present a single perspective? They believe that simplifying instruction and training materials is necessary for conveying ideas to beginners. They believe that concepts have to be simplified in order to make them understandable—in order to build on the limited, relevant world knowledge that novices possess. Such an approach, however, prevents students from being able to develop more complex and flexible knowledge structures that are required for solving ill-structured problems.

Instruction most often oversimplifies content by employing simplified prototypical examples, cases, and analogies. These are easier for the teacher or professor to think of and implement. Domain content is thus organized in predetermined knowledge packets that communicate the reliability and regularity of the content. Unfortunately, these prepackaged knowledge packets tend to be rigid and so cannot easily be adapted or transferred to new situations (Spiro and others, 1987). As a result, learners develop oversimplified views of the world because they are trying to apply rigid, compartmentalized knowledge in situations that cannot be accounted for by these simple knowledge structures (Spiro, Coulson, Feltovich, and Anderson, 1988).

Another problem with prepackaging knowledge is the belief that knowledge is context and content independent—that knowledge or skills, once acquired, easily transfer to different contexts. This belief has dominated formal instruction for a century. However, virtually every contemporary theory of learning argues the contrary: that ideas have little, if any, meaning unless and until they are embedded in some authentic context. Rather than teaching abstract rules and principles, instruction should elaborate contexts and teach ideas only in those contexts, because understanding developed in authentic contexts is better retained, more generative and meaningful, and the transfer of that learning is broader and more accurate (Spiro and others, 1987).

Computers provide the opportunity to build rich, adaptive learning environments that can reduce the effects of oversimplification. One of the best models for organizing environments to support ill-structured problem solving, especially case analysis problems, is cognitive flexibility theory (Spiro and Jehng, 1990; Spiro and others, 1987). Cognitive flexibility theory avoids oversimplifying instruction, accentuates the role of context, and stresses the conceptual interrelatedness of ideas so as to reflect the complexity that normally faces practitioners who regularly solve ill-structured problems. In order to do that, cognitive flexibility theory uses hypertext to convey multiple perspectives or interpretations of the content that it seeks to teach. It conveys multiple perspectives because there are few, if any, universal truths. Rather, given almost every idea or phenomenon, there are multiple viewpoints from which to examine it. Those viewpoints may be personal perspectives from stakeholders, disciplinary perspectives such as politics or economics, or thematic perspectives that interconnect the personal or disciplinary perspectives, such as conflict versus cooperation, isolationism versus globalization, or secularism versus religiosity.

In order to depict how learners should examine these various perspectives and themes, Spiro and others (1987; Spiro, Coulson, Feltovich, and Anderson, 1988) borrow the rich metaphor of "criss-crossing the landscape" from Ludwig Wittgenstein. The learner criss-crosses the intellectual landscape of the content domain by looking at it from multiple perspectives or through multiple themes.

Cognitive flexibility theory also emphasizes case-based instruction. Rather than basing instruction on a single example or case, it is important that learners examine a variety of real-world authentic cases by criss-crossing them through different perspectives and themes. In order to construct useful knowledge structures, learners need to compare and contrast the similarities of and differences between cases and among perspectives. The more varied these cases are, the broader are the conceptual bases that they are likely to support.

In the process of reconciling multiple perspectives on authentic cases, learners must construct their own interpretation of the truth. Rather than transmitting objective knowledge and requiring learners to encode those representations into memory, learners should be responsible for constructing their own knowledge representations. If they do not, they will never be able to adapt and use them in novel situations. Solving ill-structured problems requires intellectual flexibility that cannot be learned by memorizing any single interpretation of reality.

I next describe three examples of cognitive flexibility environments that could be used to help learners solve more complex and ill-structured problems.

Understanding Sexual Harassment

We developed a cognitive flexibility hypertext on sexual harassment for students in a speech communications class. Sexual harassment is a fuzzy concept. Traditional instructional strategies, such as lecture and class discussion, are inadequate for helping students understand the complex nature of sexual harassment and to recognize the types of it that they might encounter in their lives. Solving sexual harassment problems is thus a very ill-structured kind of problem. The goals for the hypertext were to help students recognize when they are a victim of sexual harassment, to help them become more aware of how their own actions may contribute to an environment conducive to sexual harassment, and to help them develop the ability to determine an appropriate course of action if they should encounter a situation involving sexual harassment.

The hypertext was guided by the belief that the themes and perspectives surrounding sexual harassment should be interconnected throughout the cases and that the cases needed to be authentic, believable, and perceived as actual problems to first-year university students. Students may choose to examine any of six sexual harassment cases. Some of the cases explore interactions between university personnel and students, while others involve interactions between students. Some cases explore rather straightforward situations such as sexual advances, while others deal with less obvious situations that may involve sexual harassment, such as classroom comments. The scenarios were written in such a way as to allow students, regardless of gender, to identify with several perspectives in the case. For each scenario, differing viewpoints, including those of friends, university personnel, and legal counsel, are made available to help the student understand the situation (see Figure 5–7).

Figure 5–7. Cognitive Flexibility Hypertext on Sexual Harassment.

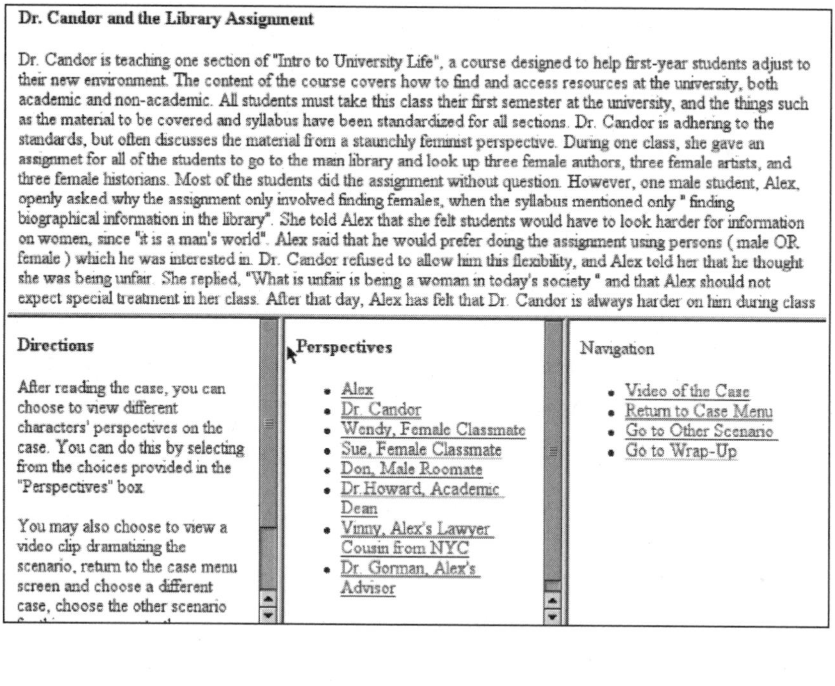

Dr. Candor and the Library Assignment

Dr. Candor is teaching one section of "Intro to University Life", a course designed to help first-year students adjust to their new environment. The content of the course covers how to find and access resources at the university, both academic and non-academic. All students must take this class their first semester at the university, and the things such as the material to be covered and syllabus have been standardized for all sections. Dr. Candor is adhering to the standards, but often discusses the material from a staunchly feminist perspective. During one class, she gave an assignmet for all of the students to go to the main library and look up three female authors, three female artists, and three female historians. Most of the students did the assignment without question. However, one male student, Alex, openly asked why the assignment only involved finding females, when the syllabus mentioned only "finding biographical information in the library". She told Alex that she felt students would have to look harder for information on women, since "it is a man's world". Alex said that he would prefer doing the assignment using persons (male OR female) which he was interested in. Dr. Candor refused to allow him this flexibility, and Alex told her that he thought she was being unfair. She replied, "What is unfair is being a woman in today's society " and that Alex should not expect special treatment in her class. After that day, Alex has felt that Dr. Candor is always harder on him during class

Directions	Perspectives	Navigation
After reading the case, you can choose to view different characters' perspectives on the case. You can do this by selecting from the choices provided in the "Perspectives" box	• Alex • Dr. Candor • Wendy, Female Classmate • Sue, Female Classmate • Don, Male Roomate • Dr. Howard, Academic Dean • Vinny, Alex's Lawyer Cousin from NYC • Dr. Gorman, Alex's Advisor	• Video of the Case • Return to Case Menu • Go to Other Scenario • Go to Wrap-Up
You may also choose to view a video clip dramatizing the scenario, return to the case menu screen and choose a different case, choose the other scenario		

In one scenario, a student's expression of wanting the freedom to research his own interests and express ideas freely in class, despite a perceived hostile attitude on the part of the professor, is the primary issue. It raises the issue of individual freedom versus the control of a person in authority, and the user may choose to follow a link to a page that examines this case based on the issue of freedom versus control. From there, links are available to similar perspectives in other cases. For example, a link is made to a perspective in a scenario that involves a student's desire to enter a building through the front door versus the rude comments made by a group of students sitting outside the entrance. In both instances, one person's freedom of choice is being curtailed by the fact that someone else appears to have control of the situation.

The criss-crossing from case to case allows the learners to develop a sense for the recurring themes that surround sexual harassment cases: freedom versus control, inclusion versus exclusion, society versus the individual, reality versus perception, and avoidance versus confrontation. These themes are intertwined with various realms—psychology, ethics, and constitutional law, to name a few—to explore sexual harassment more fully.

Freedom of Expression

The prevalence of mass media, multiculturalism, the debate over the role of government, and differing views on societal behavior has only increased the controversy concerning the limits of free expression. This flexibility hypertext describes four cases that represent a sampling of this debate. In addition to the differing perspectives of individuals involved in the situation, the environment examines each case from four thematic perspectives: freedom, censorship, public versus private funding, and community standards. The task of the student is to render a judgment about whether a legal offence has occurred (see Figure 5–8).

Figure 5–8. Case from the Flexibility Hypertext on Freedom of Expression.

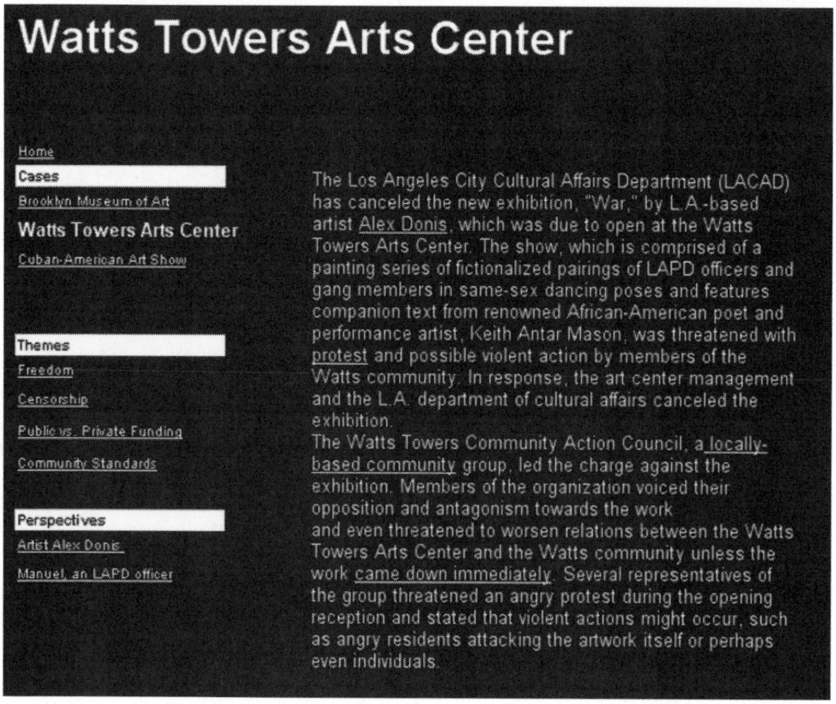

Watts Towers Arts Center

Home
Cases
Brooklyn Museum of Art
Watts Towers Arts Center
Cuban-American Art Show

Themes
Freedom
Censorship
Public vs. Private Funding
Community Standards

Perspectives
Artist Alex Donis
Manuel, an LAPD officer

The Los Angeles City Cultural Affairs Department (LACAD) has canceled the new exhibition, "War," by L.A.-based artist Alex Donis, which was due to open at the Watts Towers Arts Center. The show, which is comprised of a painting series of fictionalized pairings of LAPD officers and gang members in same-sex dancing poses and features companion text from renowned African-American poet and performance artist, Keith Antar Mason, was threatened with protest and possible violent action by members of the Watts community. In response, the art center management and the L.A. department of cultural affairs canceled the exhibition.
The Watts Towers Community Action Council, a locally-based community group, led the charge against the exhibition. Members of the organization voiced their opposition and antagonism towards the work and even threatened to worsen relations between the Watts Towers Arts Center and the Watts community unless the work came down immediately. Several representatives of the group threatened an angry protest during the opening reception and stated that violent actions might occur, such as angry residents attacking the artwork itself or perhaps even individuals.

Medical Diagnosis

Not all flexibility hypertexts address controversial topics. Jonassen, Ambruso, and Olesen (1992) described a cognitive flexibility hypertext on the practice of transfusion medicine in order to educate medical students, residents, and practicing physicians about blood banking and hemotherapy. In order to develop the hypertext, we had to articulate what it is that blood bankers do. A needs assessment showed that the primary goal of transfusion medicine for physicians is risk assessment. A matrix analysis was used to generate and structure the knowledge base, which includes fields such as the transfusion event, pathophysiology, etiology, and symptomology of that event, as well as treatments, screening tests, and so on. The causes of transfusion events may produce a variety of possible symptoms or require a variety of optional medical interventions.

The transfusion medicine hypertext includes the knowledge base; seven practice cases requiring actions that the student may take, including ordering screening tests, treating the patient, or getting more information; three test cases; and a set of twenty-four mini-cases that are related to the practice cases. In the practice cases, following the history and physical exam, students may query important operatives in the case, such as the attending physician, resident, patient, phlebotomist, or blood bank director (see Figure 5–9 for the perspective of the resident on this case); order a variety of tests; or compare the current case to similar cases that have been previously solved (see Figure 5–10).

Figure 5–9. Perspective of a Resident on a Transfusion Case.

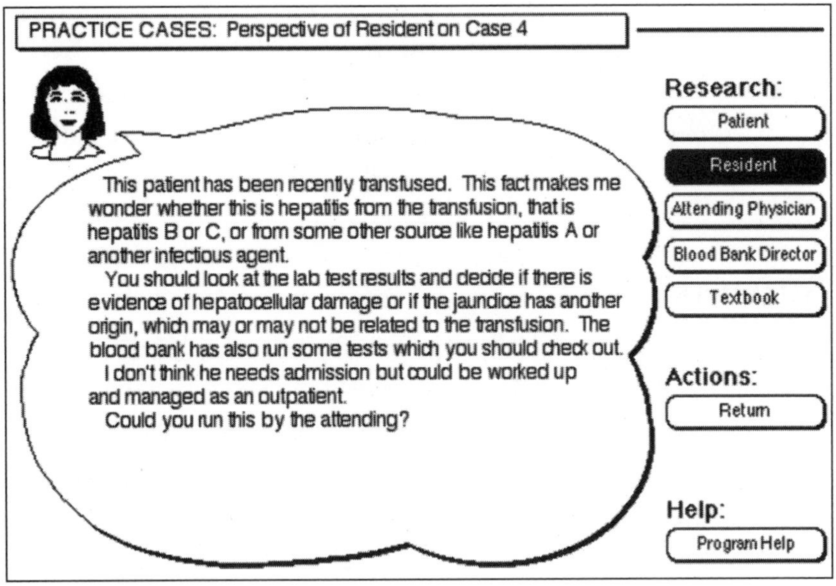

Figure 5–10. Perspective from a Previously Solved Case.

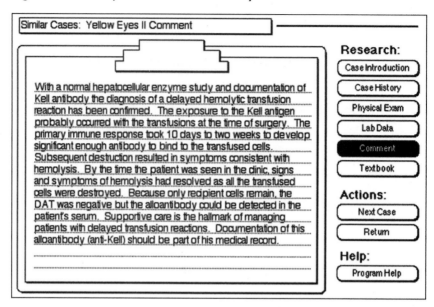

These related cases, like the perspectives and the lab results, provide a separate perspective on the case. As in real life, these perspectives often contradict each other. The performance required of the student is to manage the case. The learning task of the student is to construct an understanding of the case and the process by reconciling divergent perspectives and data.

SUMMARY

In this chapter, I have more fully described three methods for associating different solutions with different problems: worked examples, case libraries, and cognitive flexibility hypertexts. Worked examples have most often been used with well-structured story problems, so we have no evidence about their effectiveness with more ill-structured problems. Case libraries are flexible tools that have primarily been used with moderately ill-structured problems, such as diagnosis solution and decision making. Although there is little doubt that prior experience in solving well-structured problems, such as story problems, may also benefit from case libraries, there is no corroborating research. Cognitive flexibility hypertexts are probably useful only for supporting ill-structured problems, because they defy the nature of ill-structured problems, potentially violating students' expectations and increasing confusion. Although these are not the only methods for supporting solution generation, they are the methods that, based on research, appear to be the most powerful. As always, effectively using any strategy relies on good professional judgment.

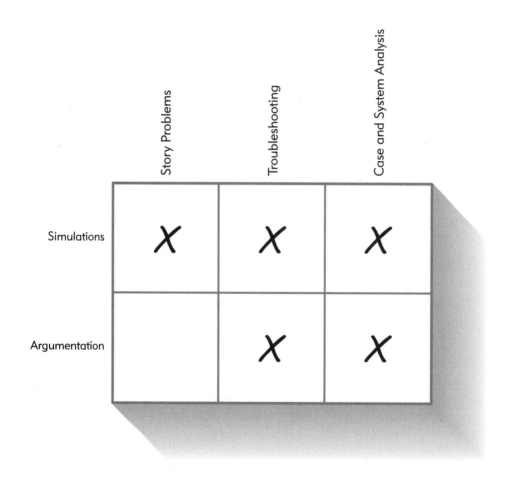

Figure 6–1. Applications of Solution Generation Methods to Problem Types.

6

Supporting Solutions

MOST GENERIC problem-solving models recommend that problems solvers clarify the problem, look for solutions, try them out, and monitor the effectiveness of the solution. Although all of these steps can be interpreted in many ways, perhaps the most problematic of them is the search for solutions. How do we search for solutions? Do we search for solutions to all problems in the same way? How do we evaluate the potential effectiveness of the solutions we have selected? Trying out and monitoring solutions to complex problems can be very expensive and even dangerous, so the search for solutions becomes even more important when tryout and monitoring is impossible. In this chapter, I describe two major methods for supporting the search for solutions: simulations and argumentation (see Figure 6–1). Other methods exist but have not been connected as closely to problem solving as these.

Simulations

Learning to solve problems requires that learners be able to manipulate the problem elements in some way, that is, manipulate parameters, make decisions, or affect the environment in some way in order to test the effects of their solutions. The form of the problem manipulation space will depend on the nature of the activity required to solve the problem. Learners should be directly engaged by the problem that they are exploring so they can experiment with the problem factors and immediately see the results of their experiments. This engagement is best supported by simulations of different kinds.

Simulations are environments where components of a system are able to be manipulated by learners. The manipulations that are available are determined by some underlying model of the system, so "the main task of the learner [is] to infer, through experimentation, characteristics of the model underlying the simulation" (de Jong and van Joolingen, 1998, p. 179). When learners interact with the simulation, they change the values of (input) variables and observe the results on the values of other (output) variables. These exploratory environments afford learners the opportunity to test the causal effects of factors (see Chapter Four for a discussion of causal reasoning). Because learners seldom have access to the underlying model, they must infer parts of the model through manipulating the environment. These are known as black box systems. The model is in a black box that cannot be seen.

There are many different kinds of simulation systems. In this chapter, I describe three different kinds of simulations that can be used to support the search for solutions during problem solving: microworlds, learning objects, and simulations.

Using Microworlds to Simulate Solutions

Microworlds are primarily exploratory learning environments, discovery spaces, and constrained simulations of real-world phenomena in which learners can navigate, manipulate or create objects, and test their effects on one another. "Microworlds present students with a simple model of a part of the world" (Hanna, 1986, p. 197). As learners interact with microworlds, they manipulate objects (or variables) in order to reach a goal state that allows them to control those phenomena and construct deeper-level knowledge of the phenomena they are manipulating. Microworlds have a feeling of direct engagement such that the student becomes immersed in the environment. Figure 6–2 illustrates the use of one microworld, ThinkerTools (White, 1993), for modeling and experimenting with principles related to trajectories in physics. This is an example of a model-using environment where the model is implicit in the environment. In ThinkerTools, the user exerts impulses on the dot prior to launching it. The relationship between the impulses or vector forces on the trajectory of the dots can be explored. In Figure 6–2, it appears that the correct vector forces were applied.

Figure 6–2. Experimenting with Principles of Trajectories in Physics Using ThinkerTools.

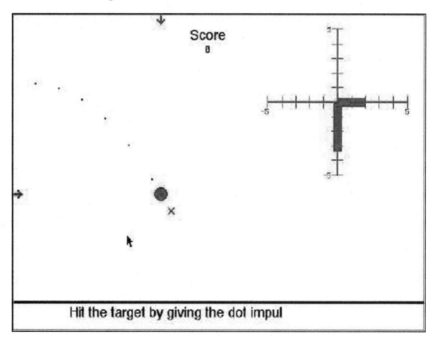

There are numerous other microworlds that can support problem solving, primarily in mathematics and the sciences. Geometer's Sketchpad is an icon-based tool for constructing geometric figures and testing relationships among the components of those figures. Genscope is an exploratory software environment in which students can solve genetics problems. In the GenScope environment, students can experiment with molecules, chromosomes, cells, organisms, pedigrees, and populations to design new creatures or manipulate existing creatures (for example, an imaginary species of dragon). Students can examine the genes of an organism (genes that control whether a dragon has wings) and then see the results of their manipulation in the organism window (a dragon sprouting wings).

MathWorlds is a microworld consisting of animated worlds and dynamic graphs in which actors move according to graphs. By exploring the movement of the actors in the simulations and seeing the graphs of their activity, students begin to understand important calculus ideas. In the MathWorlds activity illustrated in Figure 6–3, students match two motions and in the process learn how velocity and position graphs relate. Students must match the motion of the different color lines on the graphs. To do this, they can change either graph. They iteratively run the simulation to see if they got it right. Students may also use MathWorld's link to enter their own bodily motion. For example, a student can walk across the classroom, and their motions would be entered into MathWorld through sensing equipment. MathWorld would plot their motion, enabling the students to explore the properties of their own motion.

Microworlds are effective environments for enabling students to try out different solutions, but there is a limited collection of them available. Most microworlds are designed to support learning principles of science and mathematics. They have the most obvious implication for supporting the conceptual comprehension necessary for transferring story problem–solving abilities. They are normally designed and developed to meet different science standards. It will be necessary to search for available microworlds that may support the kind of problems that you are trying to support.

Figure 6–3. MathWorlds Microworld.

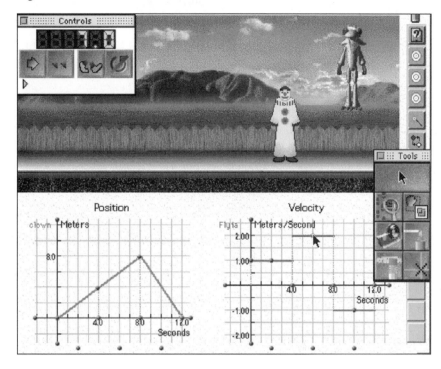

Building Learning Objects to Simulate Solutions

Learning objects are digital or nondigital entities that can be used, reused, or referenced during technology-supported learning. Learning objects may include multimedia content, instructional content, learning objectives, instructional software and software tools, and persons, organizations, and events. Their primary characteristics are reusability and rapid development of instruction.

Unlike microworlds, it is possible to build small microworld-like learning objects to support specific examples of story problem solving and even troubleshooting. A learning object is a Web-based interactive object that is used during active learning. Learning objects can provide context by illustrating parameters embedded in context. They can be used as tools, such as specialized calculators, evidence collectors, decision makers, or modeling and graphing tools. Learning objects can also provide resources, such as background information, case libraries, or databases. In this view, learning objects are catalysts for learning that must be used within some meaningful learning activity (problem solving). It is important that these learning objects are dynamic and interactive in order to allow learners to explore cause-and-effect scenarios and collect evidence to draw generalizations.

Learning objects can be created using authoring tools such as Authorware, Director, Flash, or programming platforms such as Java or JavaScript. These objects may be single use or reusable in different activities. Figure 6–4 illustrates a learning object created by Daniel Churchill (www.learnactivity.com) using Authorware and Flash. This object allows learners to test Ohm's law while trying to solve story problems using this law. Students can enter different values for the resistor or the voltage and immediately see the effects. That is, they can visualize the story problems they are trying to solve. Figure 6–5 illustrates a learning object that provides students with a suite of tools along the left that they may use when troubleshooting and repairing pump problems.

Figure 6–4. Ohm's Law Learning Object.

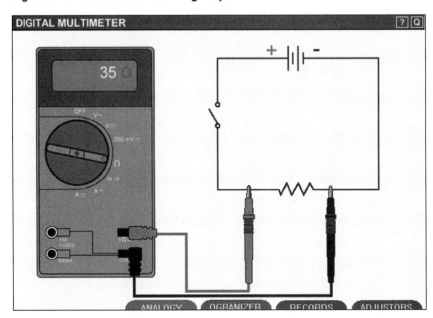

Figure 6–5. Pump Learning Object.

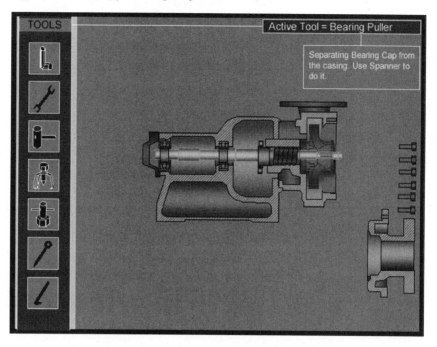

In principle, learning objects can be complex. In practice, however, because they are designed to be reusable, the scope of most learning objects is limited. These learning objects are problem specific, and they are about as complex as most learning objects ever get.

Building Simulations of Problems

Simulations, re-creations of real-world environments or phenomena, were used in classrooms for many years prior to the introduction of computers. Group activities in which learners assume different roles, such as mock trials or historical debates, can simulate real-world activities that require different kinds of problem solving. There are also sophisticated equipment simulators that realistically resemble aircraft cockpits, truck cabs, tank controls, and space shuttles. These simulators are so complex and realistic that the Federal Aviation Administration certifies pilots based on simulator experience. They enable pilots to experience and react to catastrophic events that they are likely never to experience. Several cases have been documented where simulator experiences saved planeloads of people.

A search of the Internet will produce hundreds of commercially available educational simulations (there are thousands of commercial simulation games available, most involving battles with unearthly creatures). It is possible that simulations supporting the kind of problem solving that you need may be available. Excellent examples of such simulations include Astronomy Village and BioBlast, developed by NASA's Classroom of the Future.

Figure 6–6 illustrates a BioBlast simulation of a plant biology laboratory in space where students become scientists trying to feed a space colony while recycling waste products in the process. In the figure, students set the environmental conditions under which different plants are grown. They have to

Figure 6–6. Setting Environmental Conditions in a BioBlast Simulation.

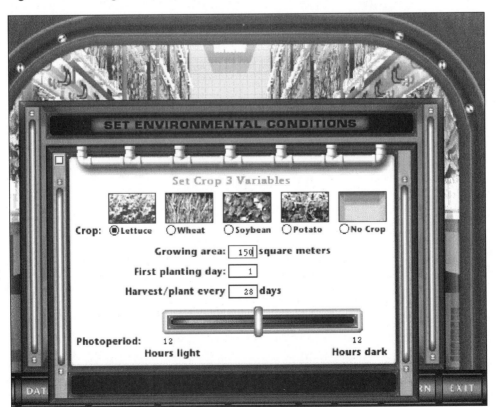

reconcile the energy used to grow the plants with the biomass produced. Students receive results on water, oxygen, and energy used and biomass produced, which they must compare with a database of human nutritional needs. They must abandon preconceptions in order to be able to feed the space colony.

When such simulations exist, they should be used judiciously to support learning how to solve problems. When they are not available (the more likely condition), then simulations need to be created. Building simulations can be a complex design and development activity. Fortunately, a number of systems have been created to help develop simulations. Systems modeling tools like Stella and PowerSim (described in Chapter Four) can be used to design and produce sophisticated Web-based simulations. Other simulation-building tools are also available. Ton de Jong at the University of Twente in the Netherlands has developed an effective simulation builder called SimQuest (www.simquest.to.utwente.nl).

Using SimQuest, authors have built a simulation of a sewage plant (Figure 6–7). The application is part of a series of courses about wastewater technology

Figure 6–7. Simulation of a Sewage Plant.

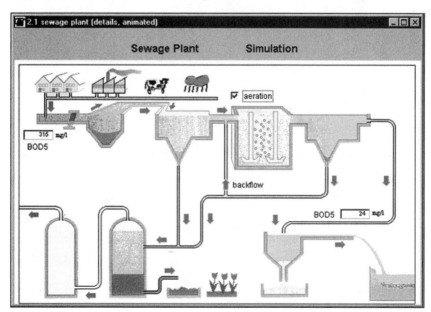

and can be used as the starting and end point of such a course. The students in this simulation get to operate a working sewage plant. This simulation may be useful in learning how to troubleshoot problems in such a plant.

Case analysis problems are more difficult to simulate, because they are usually complex and many of the factors cannot be quantified so they cannot be simulated in a quantitatively modeled simulation. Simulating case analysis problems relies on complex causal reasoning; however, the kind of causal reasoning in case analysis problems is usually modeled using qualitative representations (see Chapter Four) rather than the quantitative models that underlie story problems and troubleshooting problems. Therefore, these kinds of simulations must be constructed using a qualitative model of the factors and interactions that are specific to the problem being solved. In a problem-based learning environment on consensus building that we built (which a needs assessment showed to be the most needed skill for technology coordinators), the student attends a short meeting in the superintendent's office, where the superintendent charges the learner with the following tasks:

Hello there! I'm Judith Johnson, the Superintendent of the school district. Thanks for coming! We are having some serious disagreements in our Technology Committee meeting today about whether or not our school should provide the Internet as a resource to the students during class this year. I sure hope you can help the meeting members reach some common ground.

I have another meeting, so I need to run. When you think you've helped the group reach agreement on this issue, please send me your notes on the strategies you used. Good luck!

The student in this environment enters the simulated meeting room (Figure 6–8) where she or he gets to meet and interact with the committee. In the meeting room, the student can get background information on each of the committee members and advice from the coach before selecting what to say to the committee. The interaction in this simulated environment is between the student and the virtual committee.

Figure 6–8. The Meeting Room in a Consensus-Building Simulation.

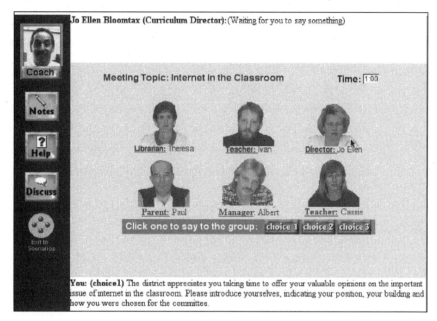

The student at each time frame in the simulation has a choice of things to say to the committee. Each choice usually pleases some of the members (they smile) and displeases others (they frown). We could have added meters to each of the committee members, such as attention, anxiety, or satisfaction, to indicate their state of mind at any point in the negotiations. In this simulation of a meeting, the learners become engaged, which is vital to meaningful learning.

Using Versus Building Simulations

It is important to distinguish between simulation using and simulation building (Alessi, 2000). Every simulation is based on a model of some kind (more often quantitative). When students use simulations, they input data and manipulate the system characteristics, testing the effects of theory manipulations. These exploratory environments afford learners the opportunity to test the causal effects of manipulations, but the underlying model that defines the system parameters is not revealed to the learner. Learners must infer the model through manipulating the environment.

In Chapter Four, I described the process of simulation building. Using modeling tools, students construct simulations of systems. Constructing and testing the system model is a complex and engaging process. Designers can also use the systems modeling software described in Chapter Four to construct simulations for students to use rather than having the learners construct the simulations. For many instructional environments, it is too time-consuming to have students construct the simulations, so providing simulations that students can manipulate can support the testing of solutions.

Argumentation

In order to solve any kind of problem, learners must state a premise (a proposed solution), which must be supported by evidence. Justifying solutions through argumentation may be the most powerful strategy available: "It is in argument that we are likely to find the most significant way in which higher order thinking and reasoning figure in the lives of most people. Thinking as argument is implicated in all of the beliefs people hold, the judgments they make, and the conclusions they come to; it arises every time a significant decision must be made. Hence, argumentative thinking lies at the heart of what we should be concerned about in examining how, and how well, people think" (Kuhn, 1992, pp. 156–157).

Argumentation is not only an essential cognitive skill; it is endemic in our culture. Postman (1995) observed that the Declaration of Independence was composed as an argument. The U.S. Constitution is also an argument, founded on the belief that every person should be allowed to freely argue his or her position.

The everyday meaning of *argument* implies conflict or a confrontation between people. But here we are looking at the term in a different way. An intellectual argument consists of two required parts: a premise and a conclusion. Arguments are normally stated in an if-then form: if (because, given that) the premise, then (therefore, consequently) the conclusion. Here is an example: "Because the biology course requires more homework than any other course, you should not take the course." This argument has an unstated assumption: that the goal of the student is to avoid excess work. A counter-argument might state, "Because you will do more work, you will learn more," followed by, "If you learn more in the biology course, then you should take it," assuming that the goal of the student is to learn as much as possible.

Argumentation Skills

Argumentation skills include analyzing arguments in text or other learning environments and the skills of constructing arguments (Marttunen, 1994). Undergraduate students are usually poor at both skills. However, solving any problem requires that the solver implicitly or explicitly construct arguments. Stated differently, the solution to any problem is an argument, that is, problem solving requires argumentation. Any solution to a problem is a conclusion. The quality of the solution (conclusion) is a function of the soundness of the premises. Argumentation is a process of making claims (drawing conclusions) and providing justification (premises) for the claims using evidence (Toulmin, 1958). It is an essential kind of informal reasoning that is central to the intellectual ability required for solving problems, making judgments and decisions, and formulating ideas and beliefs (Kuhn, 1991). Argumentation requires problem solvers to identify various alternative perspectives, views, and opinions; develop and select a preferred, reasonable solution; and support the solution with data and evidence (Voss, Lawrence, and Engle, 1991). Argumentation is a variable that significantly predicts students' performance in both well-structured and ill-structured problems (Hong, Jonassen, and McGee, 2003).

Despite its importance, most people are not adept at constructing cogent arguments (Cerbin, 1988). Specifically, they do not connect *evidence* (for example, a decrease in savings last year and an increase in sales tax revenue) to *claims* (that a tax cut will increase savings) via *warrants* (a marginal propensity to consume), but reasoning from claims to evidence is essential for problem solving. Bell and Linn (2000) suggest that conjecturing with warrants, as opposed to descriptions, in order to support arguments indicates that students are making scientific conjectures, which enables them to generate better problem solutions.

How then do we facilitate learners' development of argumentation skills? Cerbin (1988) proposed direct instruction of reasoning skills based on an explicit model of argumentation, an approach that has been the standard method for years and supported by several researchers (Knudson, 1991; Sanders, Wiseman, and Gass, 1994; Yeh, 1998). However, research findings show inconsistent results: direct instruction does not always improve argumentation skills as expected. Some research indicates that direct instruction enhances argumentation skills (Sanders, Wiseman, and Gass, 1994), whereas other research demonstrates no positive effects for direct instruction on improving argumentation skills (Knudson, 1991).

Argumentation Technologies

For the past decade, a number of researchers have been developing technology-based argumentation tools that can be used as stand-alone environments or embedded in more complex learning environments. These tools belong to a new class of cognitive tools known as computer-supported collaborative argumentation (CSCA) software. The purpose of this software is to scaffold students' construction of arguments, including seeking of warrants and evidence for supporting claims. They are structured environments for engaging students in "dialogue games" (Moore, 2000). Dialogue games have a set of rules that regulate participants' contributions to any discussion. CSCA tools are used to moderate on-line discussions.

CSCA environments can be used to support the search for solutions to different kinds of problems. When students collaborate to solve problems, they can use CSCA environments to help them construct, justify, and debate their chosen solutions. Because students are not adept at argumentation, the discussion environments can direct or scaffold more argumentative forms of discussion. Cho and Jonassen (2002) showed that the use of Belvedere (a CSCA tool to be described later) to scaffold student argument construction substantially improved not only their argumentation but also their problem-solving performance in both well-structured and, especially, ill-structured problems. Most of the environments that I describe next cannot be adapted to meet the needs of particular kinds of problem. That is, they have a set structure. Belvedere, for instance, has four predefined conversation nodes ("hypothesis," "data," "principles," and "unspecified") and three links ("for," "against," and "and") to connect those nodes. This generic structure can enhance problem solving. What is not known is how much more problem solving could be enhanced with a tailorable set of nodes and links. That capability is provided in the first tool that I will describe.

At the University of Missouri, we have constructed a scaffolded argumentation environment that allows any instructor to construct a domain-specific or problem-specific discourse structure to constrain dialogue during a discussion forum. The instructor defines the message types that are most appropriate to the discussion topic. In Figure 6–9, the instructor has identified the first message type, a Solution Proposal. This message type would be at the top level of a discussion focused on the solving a problem.

Figure 6–9. Creating Message Types.

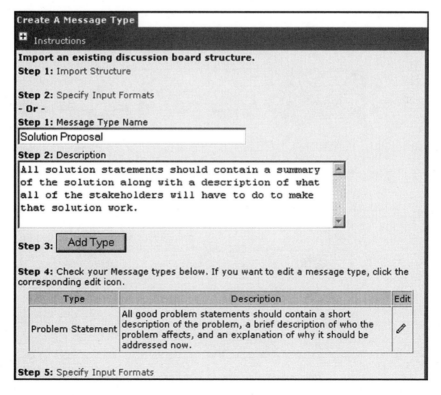

After specifying all of the message types, the instructor specifies the relationships between message types (see Figure 6–10) by checking which message types are allowed to respond to other message types. Using Toulmin's argument structure, this instructor grouped the types of statements that compose an argument into three levels (proposal, warrant, and evidence). The instructor posts a problem statement, to which students can respond using only proposal-level statements. The only statement available at the proposal level in our structure is the Solution Proposal, and it can be responded to only with warrant-level statements. Warrant-level statements are "Reason to Support," "Reason to Reject," and "Modify Proposal." The instructor may instead select theoretical warrants or warrants based on reading or accepted positions. Warrant-level statements can be responded to only with evidence-level statements, which (in this case) included "Information or Facts," "Personal Opinion or Belief," "Personal Experience," and "Research Findings." The message types can easily be changed, with others added or some deleted.

Figure 6–10. Defining Relationships Between Message Types.

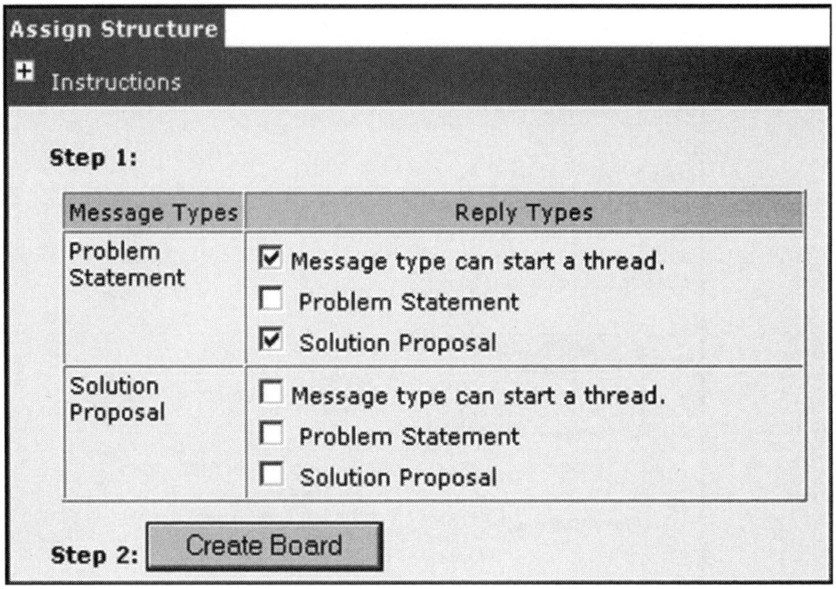

The discussion forum appears much like other threaded bulletin boards (Figure 6–11). Each hierarchically listed message can be accessed by double-clicking on it. During the on-line discussion, students could select the "New Message" link, at which point they only had the option of posting a Solution Proposal. The student could also reply to an existing message. After choosing the message to reply to and before composing the message, the student must select the message type he or she wants to post. For example, if the student is replying to a Solution Proposal message type, the first task is to choose a message type using the interface presented in Figure 6–12.

After selecting the type of message they want to post, students composed their messages. Each message is identified by message type, author, and date

---

Figure 6–11. Scaffolded Discussion Board.

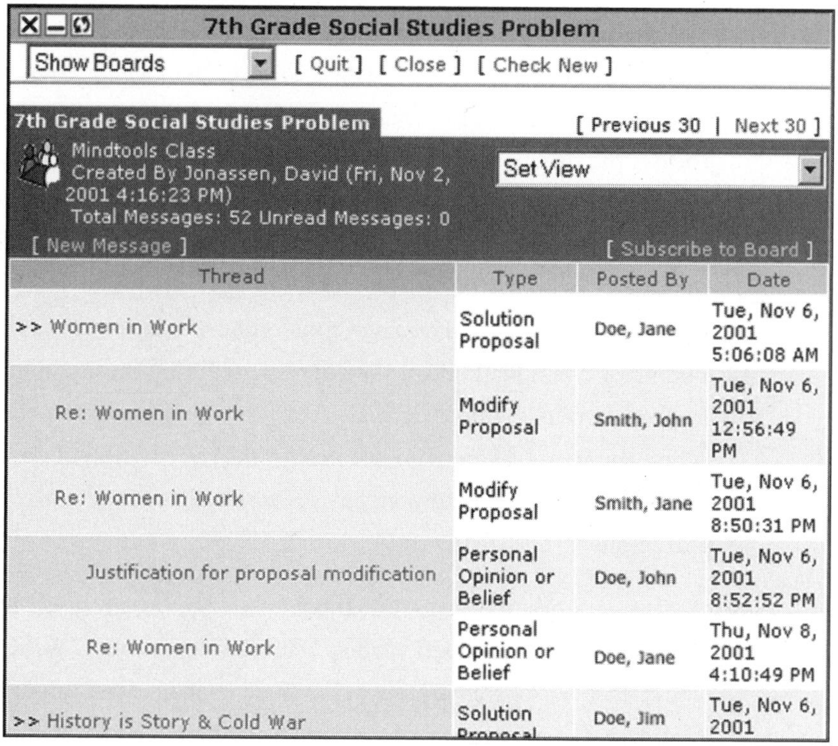

Figure 6–12. Options for Replying to a Solution Proposal.

New Message	
Step 1: Choose a Message Type.	

	Type	Description
○	Reason to Support Proposal	A principle or theory for supporting a proposed solution. At this level, you want to focus on why the proposal is a good idea. At the next level down (evidence level), anyone can provide evidence to support your reasons for supporting it.
○	Reason to Reject Proposal	A principle or theory for rejecting a proposed solution. That is, why won't this proposal work, or why isn't it a good idea? At this level, you want to focus on why the proposal is not a good idea. At the next level down (evidence level), anyone can provide evidence to support your reasons for rebutting or rejecting the proposal.
○	Modify Proposal	These messages should attempt to amend or modify the proposal. You may think that the proposal is a good idea but would be better if it were changed in some way. Suggest changes that you would support and why you believe that your changes are reasonable. At the next level down (evidence level), anyone can provide evidence to support your reasons for clarifying or changing the proposal.

Step 2: [Next >>]

(see Figure 6–11). We have field-tested this environment and are currently conducting research with it to test its efficacy.

This conversation environment allows the teacher or course designer to adapt the structure of the discussion to meet the specific needs of the activity. For example, if an instructor is designing a collaborative troubleshooting course, the discussion board could be structured according to the troubleshooting process. At the top level, students could decide which action should be taken. Elaborating on that node, lower-level nodes would require students to post a hypothesis, evidence that suggests that action, or some justification for taking that action. In teaching students how to argue before the court, the instructor could scaffold that activity by providing the argument at the top level, elaborated by precedential cases, strategic purpose, or connectives to other arguments. There is no research on the effectiveness of domain-specific conversation systems; however, it is reasonable to suspect that they will be successful.

SenseMaker. SenseMaker is part of the Knowledge Integration Environment, replaced by the Web-based Inquiry Science Environment (WISE), a free online science learning environment for students in grades 4 through 12. Sense-Maker was designed to promote middle and high school students' theorizing, support evidence-theory coordination, and make their thinking visible during classroom debate. Students group evidence items into categories and create scientific arguments that are associated with a project. Within the software, students work with evidence dots representing individual pieces of evidence on the Web and claim frames corresponding to conceptual categories (or groupings) for the evidence. (Figure 6–13 shows a SenseMaker screen.)

Figure 6–13. SenseMaker Screen.

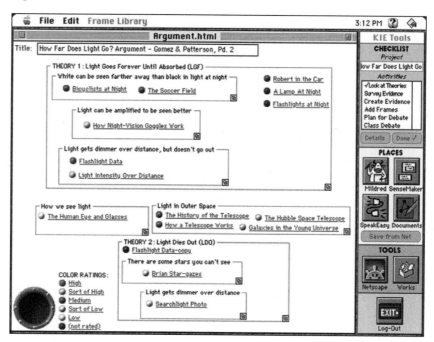

Belvedere. Belvedere was developed by the Learning Research and Development Center at the University of Pittsburgh to support students in the creation of socially constructed arguments. It provides a framework for organizing, displaying, and recording the argumentation process, so that students can easily develop their argument toward solving a problem as they work with group members.

Belvedere provides four predefined conversation nodes ("hypothesis," "data," "principles," and "unspecified," each with a different shape) and three links ("for," "against," and "and") (see Figure 6–14). Constraints in this system are

Figure 6–14. Diagram by Tenth-Grade Students on an HIV/AIDS Issue.

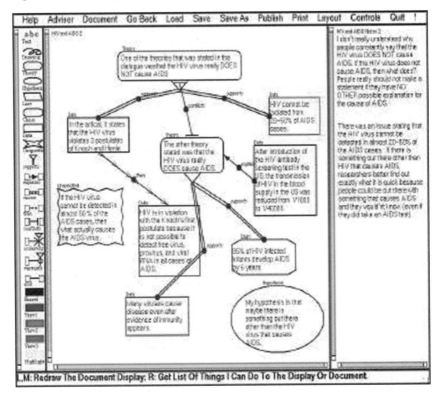

determined by the types of nodes and the links between them. Users are required to link their comments to an already existing comment using one of the four message types. For example, data and principles are meant to modify hypotheses. Students use these predefined boxes and links to develop their arguments during a problem-solving session. Students would use the tool to organize their ideas and the messages that they posted to the bulletin board system.

Convince Me. Convince Me is a domain-independent "reasoner's workbench" program that supports argument development and revision and provides feedback about how coherent arguments are based on the theory of explanatory coherence (Ranney and Schank, 1998). Convince Me incorporates tools for diagramming an argument's structure and modifying one's arguments and belief ratings. Using Convince Me, individuals can (1) articulate their beliefs

about a controversy, (2) categorize each belief as either evidential or hypothetical, (3) connect their beliefs in order to support or reject a thesis, (4)
provide ratings to indicate the believability of each statement, and (5) run
a connectionist simulation that provides feedback about the coherence of
their arguments. This feedback makes Convince Me among the most powerful argumentation tools available.

In Figure 6–15, a subject adds a belief related to the abortion controversy—
"We kill some criminals (the death penalty)"—and classifies it as reliable

---

Figure 6–15. Screen Shot of an Argumentation Environment, Convince Me.

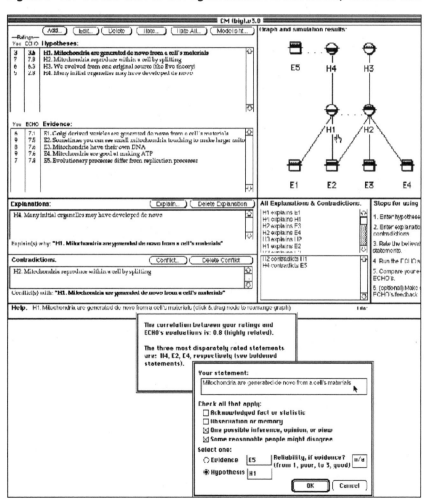

evidence (bottom) in response to Convince Me's feedback (in the middle). Proposition H4, a central node, is highlighted in the main screen area.

Convince Me has been used by subjects to reason about social situations, such as interpretations of human behavior (for example, whether yawning indicates a subconscious display of aggression or just a lack of oxygen) and whether the use of marijuana should be legalized. Using Convince Me helped students structure arguments that were consistent with their beliefs (Schank and Raney, 1992), as they changed their argument structures twice as much as students using written protocols. The Convince Me students also employed more explanations and contradictions in their arguments.

SUMMARY

In this chapter, I have explored two approaches to help students search for and test solutions. The first is to embed simulations of the problems that learners are solving in the learning environment. These simulations can be microworlds, learning objects, and model-based simulations of larger systems.

An easier and perhaps more effective way for assessing the potential effectiveness of a solution is to require learners to justify their solutions, that is, construct an argument that proves the validity of the solution that they chose. Argumentation can be used to support solution finding for any kind of problem solving, although it may be more important to learning to solve ill-structured problems. Historically, we have tried to teach generalized skills, like argumentation and critical thinking, to students in the hope that they would be able to employ them in some circumstance. There is little support for that belief. Rather than deductively teaching argumentation and requiring students to apply argumentation in different contexts, I recommend that students use one of the computer-based argumentation tools described in this chapter to help them construct coherent justifications for their solutions. As I show in Chapter Eight, argumentation is also a powerful means for assessing problem-solving skills.

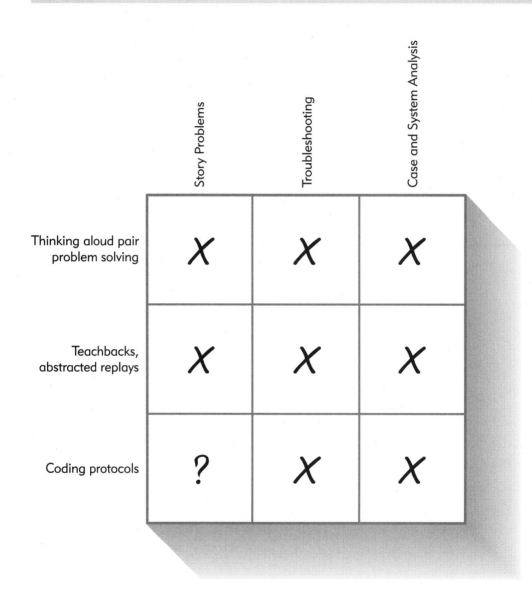

Figure 7–1. Applicability of Reflection Methods to Problem Types.

7

Reflecting on Problem-Solving Processes

FROM AN ACTIVITY theory perspective, learning requires practice (Jonassen, 2002). Practice engages learning. But practice alone is insufficient for meaningful learning and problem solving. Meaningful learning includes reciprocal intention–action–reflection cycles (see Figure 7–2). Intentionality, activity, and reflection are essential for meaningful learning and

Figure 7–2. Learning Processes and Interactions from a Constructivist Perspective.

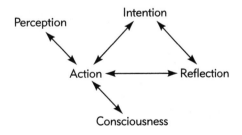

problem solving, especially in complex and new domains. Although individuals do learn some things incidentally and even accidentally without intention, action, and reflection, those learning instances tend not to be transferable.

Humans are distinct from primates in their abilities to articulate intentions and willfully plan to act on them. Meaningful learning normally results from a question, a curiosity, a perturbation, an expectation failure, or some other dissonance between what is perceived and what is understood. When that dissonance occurs, learners seek to understand the phenomena in a way that resolves that dissonance. Learning is oriented by an intention to resolve the dissonance, answer the question, satisfy the curiosity, or figure out the system. Articulating intentions is a conscious process. Articulating intentions also engages reflection by the learner on what is known and needs to be known.

Actions are the central learning mechanism. They can be physical, mental, and social all at once and typically comprise perception-action processes. Ecological psychology claims that learning results from the reciprocal perception of affordances from the environment and actions on the environment (Young, Barab, and Garrett, 2000). So learning activity involves perception-action processes (as noted by the links between perception and action in Figure 7–2). Activity theory (Jonassen, 2000c, 2002) claims that actions and consciousness are completely interactive and interdependent. We cannot act without thinking or think without acting.

In previous chapters, I have shown how to design instruction to help learners be intentional and active while they are learning to solve problems. The assumption of this chapter is that another necessary condition for meaningful learning and problem solving is reflection. Schema theorists argued that reflection is necessary to accommodate any new knowledge with what we already know. Reflection is also necessary for regulating activity, that is, reflecting on the perceptual and conscious actions that we take. Why? While perceiving and experiencing their environment, humans intentionally act on it. The perception-action and conscious-action processes engaged in by experience are the basis for reflection. Those reflections become part of the experience that is used to help explain new experiences and generate fresh intentions. Conscious activity is guided by intentions and reflections. The dialectic between reflections and intentions accounts for metacognitive activities and self-regulatory efforts engaged in by learners. Reflection is necessary for regulating learning and constructing meaning based on intentions and actions.

In this chapter, I describe reflective activities that seem particularly appropriate for helping students learn to solve problems. I assume that the ability to transfer problem-solving abilities relies on students' reflection on the intentions, processes, and actions that they took while trying to solve the problem. Each of the techniques briefly described in this chapter comes from a qualitative research tradition. That tradition calls into question their general applicability to a range of problem-solving situations. Only research can confirm that.

Peer Instruction and Thinking-Aloud Pair Problem Solving

The first pair of reflection methods requires students to articulate their thought processes while solving problems. Peer instruction engages students in teaching each other, while think-alouds engage students in personal articulation.

Peer Instruction

Concerned that students in his Harvard physics classes were learning recipes rather than conceptual understanding, Eric Mazur (1997) developed a method called peer instruction to deepen the conceptual understanding of the physics content. Rather than presenting content-based lectures to his classes, he presents problem questions that focus student attention on underlying concepts. In these questions, students are not required to solve the problem using any kind of formula. Rather, he presents questions that focus on important concepts in physics, cannot be solved by using equations, have multiple-choice answers, are unambiguously worded, and are not too easy or too difficult. Here is a sample question on Newton's third law:

A locomotive pulls a series of wagons. Which is the correct analysis of this situation?

1. The train moves forward because the locomotive pulls forward slightly harder on the wagons than the wagons pull backward on the locomotive.
2. Because action always equals reaction, the locomotive cannot pull the wagons—the wagons pull backward just as hard as the locomotive pulls forward, so there is no motion.
3. The locomotive gets the wagons to move by giving them a tug during which the force on the wagons is momentarily greater than the force exerted by the wagons on the locomotive.
4. The locomotive's force on the wagons is as strong as the force of the wagons on the locomotive, but the friction force on the locomotive is forward and large while the backward frictional force on the wagons is small.
5. The locomotive can pull the wagons forward only if it weighs more than the wagons.

Mazur poses the question and gives the students one minute to formulate an answer. All students record their answers and their level of certainty about their answer (an easy but effective metacognitive prompt). Students must then spend a couple of minutes convincing their neighbors of the correctness of their answer, after which each student may revise his or her answer. If a significant portion of the students still have the wrong answer, Mazur attempts to explain the question. Convincing neighbors is most effective when only half of the students initially get the question correct. Many more students change their answers from incorrect to correct than the opposite.

Mazur has conducted research on the effectiveness of peer instruction and found that conceptual understanding of physics improves dramatically, as do problem-solving skills. This research shows the importance of conceptual understanding of domain concepts to problem-solving performance. From a teaching perspective, peer instruction is valuable because the teacher has immediate feedback on student understanding.

Peer instruction is described as an in-class, face-to-face strategy. It would be difficult, though not impossible, to apply it to on-line instruction as well, especially in environments where synchronous discussions and grouping are possible. How well peer instruction works in asynchronous environments is not known. Clearly, peer instruction provides numerous opportunities for research.

Thinking-Aloud Pair Problem Solving

Thinking-aloud pair problem solving (TAPPS) is an articulation-reflection method developed and researched over the years by Whimbey and Lochhead (1999). TAPPS is a combination of think-aloud and teachback techniques. Working in pairs, one student thinks aloud while solving any problem. Thinking aloud requires the problem solver to vocalize as many of the assumptions, methods, inferences, or conclusions that she is constructing or recalling while solving a problem. Thinking aloud requires some practice; in TAPPS, it is scaffolded by the listener. The listener listens to the problem solver's vocalizations and continually checks the accuracy of the problem solver's actions or assumptions. Catching errors requires the listener to follow and understand every step that the problem solver takes. Listening also requires that the listener never let the problem solver get ahead of her own thinking. The listener may require a time-out in order to catch up. It is essential that the listener be working the problem with the problem solver, not separately. When the listener encounters an error, he simply points out the error but does not attempt to correct it. The problem solver must perform all of the work. Finally, the listener must demand constant vocalization. When the problem solver goes quiet, the listener must prompt her to vocalize what she is thinking. The listener should continue to ask questions of the problem solver to ensure that the problem solver understands what she is doing. Lochhead (2001) provides numerous examples of these interactions.

The role of listener is more difficult than the problem solver. The listener must be fully engaged in the problem-solving process. Because of the difficulty of being a listener, Whimbey and Lochhead recommend that the partners switch roles often.

Teachbacks and Abstracted Replays

Perhaps the most effective and easiest way to monitor learners' understanding is to ask them to teach back to you what you taught to them.

Teachbacks

A common method for assessing mental models is the teachback procedure, in which learners or users are asked to teach another learner (typically a novice) how to perform certain tasks or how to use a particular system. This is also a very simple reflection method for students. After some instructional activity or combination or activities, the instructor asks students to teach back what they have learned to someone else. This can be done orally or in writing.

Students can produce a variety of representations, including lists of commands, verbal descriptions of task components, flowcharts of semantic components, or descriptions of keystrokes (van der Veer, 1989). Regardless of the form of the response, these teachbacks provide the easiest and clearest assessment of student understanding that is available. Student misconceptions or inadequate conceptions stick out like the proverbial sore thumb. Their teachbacks must be interpreted, which makes assessment more difficult; however, the clarity with which they convey student comprehension makes them worth the effort. In addition to clarity, teachbacks can be easily implemented in any instructional context about any content or skills.

Abstracted Replays

Earlier in my life, I played a lot of contract bridge. With most contract bridge, more time is spent analyzing the bidding and play of the hand after the contract is over than actually playing the hand. The purpose of these analytic reflections is to develop better bidding and playing skills and also to improve nonverbal communication between partners. We would replay the bidding and the hand in order to generalize lessons from that hand to bridge-playing skills. Each partner was attempting to teach the other what he or she learned from the bidding and play of the hand. These were a form of abstracted replays. What made these replays more useful was the complexity of the game.

Bridge requires complex problem solving because of the large number of rules, their infinite combination, and the many different bidding and playing schemas that the partners negotiate.

Abstracted replay involves the review and analysis of any activity. Stopping intentionally to discuss the way that problems were conceived or solved and how successful any problem-solving attempts were is an invaluable reflection method. There are no rules or formats for abstracted replays. Those involved with the activity will make points or review processes as they perceive the need. This is a useful activity after any collaborative problem solving.

Coding Protocols

Another powerful form of reflection that can provide very meaningful instruction on problem-solving processes analyzes think-aloud protocols. In a series of studies (Atman and Bursic, 1998; Atman and Turns, 2001), students assumed the roles of researchers as they coded think-aloud protocols of problem-solving sessions. That is, rather than studying how to solve problems, they analyzed the written transcripts of problem-solving sessions conducted by other students. In other words, they learned how to solve problems by analyzing how others solved them.

These students were given the transcripts of the problem-solving sessions where other students were working in pairs to design a Ping-Pong ball launcher, a playground, or some other product. Participants in these sessions had been asked to think aloud (verbalize their thoughts) throughout their problem-solving process. The students in these studies identified message units in the protocols and classified the purpose of each message according to the following classifications:

- Identify the need for solving problem.
- Identify the problem and constraints and criteria.
- Gather information beyond that provided in the problem statement.
- Generate ideas for solutions.

- Develop a model of the problems.
- Determine the feasibility of solutions.
- Evaluate alternative solutions.
- Make a decision.
- Communicate the decision and instructions to others.
- Implement the solution, and draw implications.

These codes were generated for the study based on textbook descriptions of engineering design processes. Problem solving in different domains or different kinds of problem solving requires different classification systems. Also, different coding systems may be used to analyze the same problem-solving protocols. (In Chapter Eight, I describe another study where we used different coding schemes to assess the abilities of students to construct meaningful arguments.)

Students classified each message individually and then met with another coder to arbitrate differences between their classifications. Some differences were impossible to reconcile; however, agreement among student coders was high.

What is most significant about this process is that the students coding the transcripts were not learning about engineering design outside the practice of engineering design. That is, they were analyzing practice. That analysis helped these coders better understand the design process, appreciate the complexity and ambiguities implicit in the design process, and understand uses of alternative strategies for designing. Although the purpose of these studies was to study the coding and arbitration processes among coders, I believe that coding protocols is a powerful form of instructional support to help students to learn how to become problem solvers. How well does coding protocols transfer to problem-solving abilities? That has never been studied. There are numerous potential research issues: the number, variety, and quality of the problem solving captured in the protocols being analyzed; coding versus practice in solving problems; the effects of alternative coding schemes on problem-solving practice; and many others. Future research will likely prove the effectiveness of this coding process on problem-solving abilities.

SUMMARY

In this chapter, I have described three kinds of methods for engaging reflection on problem-solving activities. Peer instruction and thinking-aloud pair problem solving pair students up to teach each other how to solve problems. Thinking-aloud pair problem solving is probably more engaging because of the important error-checking role played by the listener. Teachbacks and abstracted replays are less formal methods for engaging learners in reviews and analysis of problem-solving activities. They do not require extensive training, but they can probably be used effectively in on-line learning environments. Finally, coding protocols is a more formal method, where students learn how to solve problems by analyzing the problem-solving processes of other problem solvers. This may be one of the most effective instructional strategies for helping students learn how to solve problems, although no research has been done to determine this. The assumption of all of the activities described in this chapter is that intentionally reflecting on how problems were solved will improve the ability of learners to solve others.

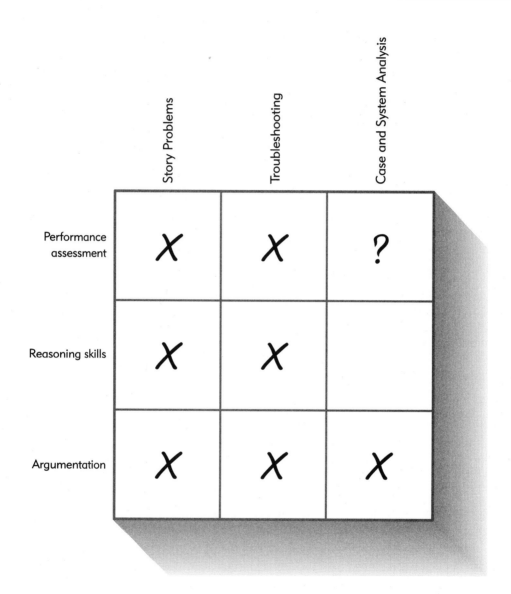

Figure 8–1. Assessing Problem Solutions and Learning.

8

Assessing Problem Solutions and Learning

ASSESSMENT IS probably the most important component in formal education. Students know that what is important is what gets assessed. Regardless of stated goals, objectives, missions, curricula, or any other descriptor of learning outcomes, what is "on the test" is what is important to students because, they believe, it is important to teachers, professors, and trainers. Unfortunately, that is not a good assumption. What is important to teachers, professors, and trainers may have little to do with the kinds of assessments they use. They hope that their students can think critically and solve problems, but often they do not know how to design and implement quality assessments of meaningful learning.

Probably the fastest way to enhance learning in schools, universities, and corporate training venues is to implement assessments that assess meaningful learning. Students would then know that meaningful learning, rather than memorization, is important. But there is another problem with quality assessments: constructing and applying meaningful assessments is a complex skill that many educators do not possess, and it is much harder work than constructing recall test items. Thus, educators have to develop these skills; moreover, meaningful learning requires more than one form of assessment. Almost every course or class in K–12, university, and corporate training uses only one form of assessment to assess learners' knowledge, skills, and abilities. Educators use multiple-choice examinations, written essays, laboratory activities, or other assessment methods. They assign grades or evaluations based on only one form of assessment of knowledge and skills. Single forms of assessment, however, betray the richness and complexity of any problem solving. Problem solving cannot be effectively assessed using only one form of assessment. Engaging students in instructional activities and assessments that employ only a single formalism for representing their knowledge necessarily restrains their understanding of whatever they are studying. Students at all levels of education have a deficient understanding of content and skills because they were required to represent what they know in only one way.

Using appropriate forms of assessment is critical to learning to solve problems. If we teach students to solve problems but assess only their ability to recall what they have memorized for a test, then they will quickly lose interest in problem solving. One of the foundational assumptions of instructional design is that the conditions of learning should match the learning outcomes that should match the assessment. Assessment needs to be congruous with the problem-solving outcomes that are taught. Adequate assessment of problem-solving skills requires more than one form of assessment. The ability to solve problems and the cognitive residue of that experience cannot be adequately assessed in only one way. There are many ways to assess problem solving. In this chapter, I describe the three forms of assessment that are most appropriate for assessing problem-solving skills:

- Assessing students' problem-solving performance

- Assessing the component, cognitive skills required to solve problems (for example, understanding of domain concepts and causal reasoning)

- Assessing students' ability to construct arguments in support of their solutions to problems

Each of these forms of assessment requires different cognitive skills. I recommend using some form of all three assessments when assessing problem solving. Instructors who want their students to learn to solve different kinds of problems must learn to teach them to solve problems and then assess their different abilities to solve the kinds of problems that they practiced. The problems should be at the same level of difficulty.

Assessing Problem-Solving Performance

The concept of performance assessment is easy: Can the students perform the task? It is not whether they remember how to solve problems and not whether they remember the domain content required to solve problems. Rather, can the students solve problems similar to the ones they have been taught? Can they perform problem solving? How well did they solve the problem?

Performance assessment includes these elements (Elliott, 1995):

- Students must construct a response or a product rather than simply select from a set of predefined alternatives or answers.

- Assessment consists of direct observation or assessment of student behavior on problem-solving tasks.

To these, I add a third:

- Assessment of the quality of the product or observation using a rubric, that is, a description of desirable performance.

Solving any kind of problem requires multiple operations or actions and different kinds of skills and knowledge. For example, oral reports in a typical classroom are mysteriously graded (neither students nor teachers can really explain the criteria for grading), and few comments generally accompany the grade. So students typically know only what grade (evaluation) they received but not which aspects of the performance were responsible for that grade. The use of rubrics will provide that information.

Constructing Rubrics

Assessing performance requires assessing each procedure, action, or skill that the students performed while solving the problem or at least a representative sampling of those actions if the problem is very complex. In order to assess performance, it is necessary to construct descriptors of the required actions, thoughts, and operations so that we know what good performance is. These descriptors are called *rubrics*.

Rubrics describe performance (good performance and bad performance). They often take the form of a scale or set of scales used to assess a complex performance that should be used to assess performance but also used to improve performance by the students. In order to construct rubrics, we start by identifying criteria for judging good performance. For example, consider the task of making an effective oral presentation. There are several criteria that can be used to assess an effective oral presentation, including (but certainly not limited to) organization, pace, vocal qualities, and use of visual aids. Although criteria are useful, interpreting them is individualistic. The rubrics need to describe the kinds of behavior or performance that operationalize each criterion in terms of good performance and bad. If we were assessing student contributions to a group discussion, for instance, one of the important criteria would be quality of student comments. What does that mean? It might look something like that in Exhibit 8–1.

Exhibit 8–1. Assessing the Quality of Comments.

Inadequate		Adequate		Exceptional
Comments ramble, distract from topic	. . . .	Comments usually pertinent, occasionally wander from topic	. . . .	Comments are always related to topic

The most effective and useful rubrics tend to display important characteristics of performance. Jonassen, Howland, Moore, and Marra (2003) articulated these criteria for a good rubric:

- *In an effective rubric, all important elements are included.* Any aspect of performance that is important enough to assess should have a scale with ratings that describe it. Rubrics identify the aspects of the performance that are considered important.

- *In an effective rubric, each element is unidimensional.* In chemistry, an *element* is irreducible. It cannot be further separated. So each rubric must describe elemental behavior. If you were assessing a student presentation, you might be interested in voice quality. Is that elemental, or is it really a combination of separate elements such as volume and intonation? Rubrics that attempt to assess combinations of elements are more difficult to use and not as meaningful.

- *In an effective rubric, ratings are distinct, comprehensive, and descriptive.* The ratings should cover the range of expected performances for each element. Rubrics should use three to seven distinct ratings. For example, the volume element in an oral presentation can be described in a range of ways: barely audible, quiet and indistinguishable, audible with effort, appropriate for the size of the room and the audience, too loud, or abusively loud. A good rubric does not default to a standard five-point scale: unacceptable, poor, acceptable, good, excellent. These evaluate the performance but do not describe the nature of the performance.

- *An effective rubric communicates clearly with the learners.* The ultimate purpose of a rubric is to improve performance. This is accomplished by clarifying expectations and providing important information about progress toward the desired goal states. Rubrics convey the complexity of the task and focus intentional learning. They provide specific feedback to learners about the nature of their performance.

Writing and using rubrics is hard work. So why do it? Being able to describe appropriate problem-solving performance is essential to supporting and assessing problem solving. Articulating proper performance is critical to making informed judgments. Most people recognize an excellent performance when they see it but often are unable to say why the performance was excellent. That is not adequate for assessment purposes.

I next exemplify rubrics for different kinds of problems. Then I will provide more advice on how to construct rubrics.

Story Problems. Most story problems require learners to understand the nature of the problem, select an appropriate formula to represent the problem, insert the values from the problem into the formula, and solve the formula for a specific value. Most story problems are assessed based on whether the student produces the correct value for an answer. Problems are normally stated in terms of story problems that are similar to the ones that students have practiced solving—in this example, a chemistry problem:

> The cryoscopic constant of water is 1.86 K/(molKg^{-1}). The addition of 100 g of compound A to 750 g of water lowered the freezing point of water to 1.4 °K. The molar mass of this compound A is
>
> a. 90 g.
> b. 100 g.*
> c. 100,000 g.
> d. 110 g.

In this example, students must calculate the answer and select the appropriate response from the multiple-choice list. Because of the nature of multiple-choice questions, the only criterion for assessment is the selection of the correct answer. However, that violates the first criterion for good rubrics: all important elements of performance are included. With multiple-choice questions, none of those elements can be observed, so multiple choice is not an appropriate format for performance assessment. Students must provide evidence of the constituent operations required to solve the problem.

A more appropriate performance problem, this one from physics, includes more contextual information and requires learners to illustrate their performance:

A policeman chases a master jewel thief across city rooftops. They are both running at 5 m/s when they come to a gap between the buildings that is 4 m wide and has a drop of 3 m. The thief, having studied a little physics, leaps at 5 m/s and at a 45-degree angle and clears the gap easily. The policeman did not study physics and thinks that he should maximize his horizontal velocity, so he leaps at 5 m/s horizontally. Does he clear the gap? By how much does the thief clear the gap? What type of problem is this? Show all actions, assumptions, and formulas used to answer these questions.

In this example, the student must classify the problem type, identify initial conditions, set up the equation, estimate the answer, and solve the equation. Rubrics can be created for assessing the student's solution method because the students are required to show their work. These operations define the nature of the required rubrics. For story problems, the primary rubric focuses on the correctness of the answer. Some possible rubrics for assessing physics problem solving are shown in Exhibit 8–2.

Exhibit 8–2. Example Rubrics for Assessing Story Problems.

Accuracy of problem classification

Misclassified problem	Identified correct group but misclassified specific problem type	Correctly classified the specific problem type

Identification of initial conditions

Unable to identify any initial or final conditions	Identified some initial or final conditions	Correctly identified all initial and final conditions in problem

Accuracy of equation

Used wrong equation or misplaced all values	Used correct equation but misplaced some values	Equation set up correctly with values in correct places

Exhibit 8–2. Example Rubrics for Assessing Story Problems, Cont'd.

Accuracy of answer estimate

Estimate of answer the wrong order of magnitude	Estimate right order of magnitude but wrong sign or not close to final answer	Estimate of answer very close to final answer

Unit consistency

Units completely mismatched	Units mixed; some correct	Correct units used and cancelled

Accuracy of answer

Answer is quite different from correct answer	Answer is close to correct answer; arithmetic operation suspected	Answer is exactly correct, to the nearest hundredths

The nature of the rubrics will differ with the domain and nature of the problem. The rubrics must address the specific performances required by the problem. These can be used only when students' responses include some evidence of their thinking.

Troubleshooting Problems. Assessing troubleshooting skill requires that learners troubleshoot problems, not remember troubleshooting procedures or take an examination about troubleshooting. There are at least two ways of doing that. One method is to introduce a bug into the kind of system that students have learned to troubleshoot and to require them to troubleshoot the system in real time with no hints, then observe and assess their performance. Another method is to have students "walk through" a troubleshooting performance explaining what they are doing and why. This method allows the teacher to probe students' performance with questions about the meaning of different actions. This think-aloud protocol analysis (see Chapter Seven) enables learners to articulate their plan for solving the problem while the teacher observes and assesses how well they adhere to the plan, what strategies they use for dealing with discrepant data and events, and what kinds of generalizable conclusions they can draw from the solution.

Jonassen and Henning (1999) described a troubleshooting study in electronics technology that used the first method. The problem was a three-phase motor simulation controlled by a three-pole motor starter that is controlled by a 208-volt coil that is switched by a line voltage cooling thermostat and switch. These components were mounted to a board and wired together. For each student, we bugged the system in some way (disconnected a wire, grounded a component, inserted defective parts, and so on). Students used visual cues and a voltmeter to determine what caused the load to be energized. We observed and timed each student while he or she troubleshot the system. The slowest troubleshooter required more than five minutes to troubleshoot the systems and indicated in the think-aloud that he "couldn't see the problem." He required consistent instructor prompting to complete the required tests, and his testing sequence was less goal oriented and systematic than that of other students. He randomly tested different parts of the system. The fastest troubleshooter tested the system systematically. He checked power first and then proceeded to check each set of connections with his voltmeter until he found the fault forty-five seconds later. The think-aloud enabled us to observe how well the students adhered to a plan, what strategies they used for dealing with discrepant data and events, and what kinds of generalizable conclusion they can draw from the solution.

In order to assess their performance, we developed the rubrics shown in Exhibit 8–3.

Exhibit 8–3. Example Rubrics for Assessing Troubleshooting.

Coherence of plan

Had no apparent plan; proceeded to troubleshoot randomly	Appeared to have a plan but diverged occasionally in process	Appeared to have a plan and used it consistently	Articulated plan and followed plan systematically

Exhibit 8–3. Example Rubrics for Assessing Troubleshooting, Cont'd.

Speed of troubleshooting performance

Required more than 15 minutes to discover fault	Identified fault area within 3–4 minutes but required more than 5 more to isolate fault	Required less than 5 minutes to isolate fault	Identified exact fault state within 2 minutes

Independence of action

Could not proceed to do anything without prompts or assistance	Started without assistance but needed help to isolate fault	Needed assistance or prompts only once or twice	Required no prompts or assistance to identify fault

Adaptiveness of performance

No way of dealing with discrepant events or results; acted randomly	Confused by any divergent results of actions; little strategic ability	Addressed divergent results or actions inconsistently; not certain of how to recover	Revised strategies to accommodate divergent information

Several other rubrics could be constructed as well. Essentially, instructors must identify the components or elements of performance that they believe are important for students to exhibit in their solution. Then they need to describe a range of actions that describe effective to ineffective performance of each element.

The exact nature of the rubrics will depend on the kind of system being troubleshot, the nature of the data collection, and hypothesis testing to solve the problem. For instance, in assessing a medical diagnosis, the rubrics required to describe that performance would vary significantly from those required to isolate an electronics fault. The system is completely different, and so are the tools used to provide case evidence.

Case Analysis Problems. Case analysis problems are everywhere. The front pages of every local and national newspaper are filled with case analysis problems. From "How do we deal with overcrowding in our local school classrooms?" to "How do we bring peace to the Middle East?" the world is filled with complex problems that require interdisciplinary solutions that consider multiple perspectives.

Here is a case analysis problem from the database of the Union of International Associations (www.uia.org):

> Water-borne diseases. Most public water supplies are routinely monitored, but private supplies may not be subject to the same quality standards. In the Russian Federation, half the population uses water that fails to meet quality standards. In Latvia, 55% of water samples from shallow wells fail to meet microbiological standards. Yet half the rural population relies on these wells as a source of drinking water. Some 50% of Armenian supplies also fail to meet quality standards. Even in countries where most residents are connected to a water supply network, there may be frequent interruptions in supply. In southern Russia, water may be available for only a few hours a day. In Romania, some supply systems do not function for more than 12 hours a day. Around 30% of Italy's islanders also suffer interruptions in their water supply. Apart from contamination with microbes and viruses, water may also be polluted with lead, arsenic, fluorides or nitrates. Agriculture also affects water quality through run-off containing pesticides and fertilizers.
>
> In Albania, 25 people died of cholera in 1994 after drinking contaminated water. In Latvia, several hundred cases of hepatitis A and bacterial dysentery are attributed to contaminated drinking water each year. In Tajikistan, some 4000 cases of typhoid fever were reported in 1996 following heavy rainfall. In the past decade there have been some 190 outbreaks of bacterial dysentery, 70 outbreaks of hepatitis A and 45

outbreaks of typhoid fever associated with drinking water and recreational water in Europe and central Asia.

In Sweden in the past decade, there have been six outbreaks of waterborne campylobacteriosis, which causes gastroenteritis. In fact, a total of 27,000 people suffered from waterborne disease in Sweden in those ten years. During the same period, the United Kingdom reported 13 outbreaks of cryptosporidiosis, which also causes gastroenteritis and can usually be traced back to agricultural pollution. More than five million people, most of them children, die every year from illnesses caused by drinking poor quality water.

It is probably not useful to pose the problem as, "What can be done about this state of affairs?" Rather, you need to contextualize the problem in some way—for example, "Advise the Secretary General of the United Nations what actions should be taken by the U.N." or "Investigate the waterborne diseases of a particular country, and make recommendations to the prime minister of that country." Students could individually or collaboratively write position papers to deliver at national councils; they could advise the president or create policy papers for the United Nations secretary general on how to deal with these problems; they could construct presentations to alert others in their communities about these problems; they could organize petitions in their own communities; they could investigate water quality in their own community; they could construct chemistry experiments to test different filtering of chemical solutions to different sources of poisoning; or they could build models of the growth of bacteria in different waterborne environments. There are literally hundreds of problems related to this general problem state.

Because of the complex nature of the problem, the assessment will depend on the nature of the specific problem posed to the students. The nature of the rubrics will depend on the nature of the task. If students were to write a policy paper for the United Nations secretary general, some rubrics for assessing the paper might include those shown in Exhibit 8–4.

Exhibit 8–4. Example Rubrics for a Case Analysis Problem.

Quality of information sources cited

Sources of information in report unknown	Sources of information in report were questionable and not well established	Sources of information in report were internationally recognized

Constraint analysis

Solution considered few, if any, social, political, and economic constraints	Many constraints identified; unequal balance among sources	All known social, political, and economic constraints identified in report

Economic feasibility

Solution recommendations are economically impossible	Solution recommendations have unclear economic implications	Solution recommendations are feasible within current economic constraints

Relevance of political implications

Few, if any, political implications identified	Political implications identified but unclear how they affect situation	Political implications are clear and feasible within current political context

Many, many other rubrics could be constructed to describe such a complex behavior, including all of the quality issues surrounding the writing of the report. The nature of the rubrics constructed to assess any activity should emphasize the aspects of the performance that you deem most important.

Most, but not all, of the rubrics described before have focused on the products of student performance. Rubrics can and should focus on both products and processes. Another way to assess case analysis problem solving is to observe and assess the problem-solving process. Audiotaping or videotaping the problem solvers while they are solving problems and transcribing those tapes provides a verbal protocol to analyze.

Atman and Turns (2001) described a series of verbal protocol studies where they observed engineering students engaged in design tasks. Design tasks are similar to case analysis problems, only they are more ill structured. Students would think aloud (Ericsson and Simon, 1993; see Chapter Seven for more discussion on think-aloud protocol and protocol analysis). They developed a series of codes including identification of need, problem definition, gathering information, generating ideas, feasibility analysis, evaluation, decision, communication, and implementation. Each thought that students uttered as they solved one of four design problems aloud was classified according to one of these codes. The analyst had to classify the purpose of the utterance based on definitions and examples. The codes that Atman and Turns used were meant to characterize the cognitive activities engaged by design problem solving. Different kinds of problem solving required different codes. Atman and Turns found that older students (seniors) identified more criteria, had significantly more transitions between design steps, and gathered more information than younger students (freshmen). Verbal protocol analysis is a more difficult kind of analysis, but it exposes student reasoning better than most other forms of assessment. After coding protocols, you really understand the students.

The verbal protocol analysis process is made easier when the discussions are on-line, because each message and its producer are already identified and the contents of the discussion forum can be saved in a database. Cho and Jonassen (2002) analyzed each of the messages posted during problem-solving sessions by classifying each message based on a problem-solving coding scheme: the Decision Function Coding System (DFCS) adapted from Poole and Holmes (1995). The DFCS consists of seven categories: problem definition, orientation, criteria development, solution development, solution approval, solution critique, and nontask statement. We found that providing a constraint-based argumentation scaffold during group problem-solving activities increased the generation of coherent arguments and that groups that solved ill-structured problems produced more extensive arguments.

The nature of the coding scheme could be changed to focus on the required elements of the problem. For instance, we could have used constraint analysis, political implications, or any other element required in the solution. These codes, in effect, represent a rubric, so the teacher is coding student responses in terms of desired behavior.

Jonassen and Kwon (2001) used a similar coding scheme to compare problem-solving processes used in computer-mediated communication versus face-to-face communication. We found greater use of nontask simple agreement (corresponding to solution approval) and simple disagreement (corresponding to solution critique) categories for both well-structured and ill-structured tasks in the computer-mediated group relative to the face-to-face group. That is, the nature of the task did not have a significant effect on the problem-solving processes that the students used. That is why Cho and Jonassen scaffolded problem-solving skills. Coding messages or interactions observed while students are problem solving provides valuable information about the nature of problem solving that students performed. Again, the emphasis in all of these methods is to analyze performance.

Heuristics for Developing an Effective Rubric

Developing rubrics is a complex task. As is the case in most complex tasks, there is no single right answer. For most activities for which a rubric might be an appropriate assessment device, it is quite likely that different people would develop different rubrics, each with its own set of advantages and shortcomings. Although there is not a single right way to develop a rubric, the following set of heuristics will help to provide some direction to initial rubric development activities. As you become more proficient, you will no doubt refine these heuristics to meet your own needs.

Start by making a list of the major elements, aspects, or components of the activity. An element is an important component of the overall task or activity. Elements listed before include economic feasibility, completeness of plan, and so on. You should create elements for every aspect of the activity that you wish to assess. Your elements should be unidimensional. That means they should be single items that cannot be reduced to a set of other items. When elements are not unidimensional, you will have a hard time defining the actual performance activities that define the element. A general rule of thumb is that you should have somewhere between three and seven elements. If you believe you need more than that, you may need to consider separate rubrics. For example, for a rubric for multimedia presentations, we might define three elements: organization, content, and delivery. For each element:

1. *Define the element.* What activities define that element? What is it you wish to see in a student's performance relative to that element? For the multimedia presentation example, we might define organization as the thoughtful structuring of the elements of the presentation in order to achieve the stated objectives.

2. *Define the rating scale for each element.* You should not necessarily use the same rating scale for all elements. Refer to the characteristics of an effective rubric for more hints on defining a rating scale. The scale should be descriptive of the element in question. For the organization of the multimedia presentation, the scale might be: inadequate, adequate, excellent.

3. *Define the meanings of the each scale item.* Each must be defined in action- or behavior-oriented terms. This is the hardest work involved in rubric creation. Clearly defining what each level of the scale means can be difficult. Here is a definition in specific action- and product-oriented terms of an inadequate organization for a multimedia presentation:

- The presentation was untitled.

- The objective was not stated.

- The objective was unclear.

- The outline or storyboard was not provided.

- The outline or storyboard provided did not match the content of the presentation.

- The speaker notes were not prepared.

- The speaker notes were present but were not well enough prepared to allow for a smooth, polished speaking role.

- Rehearse the presentation using the speaker notes until a smooth delivery is attained.

At the other end of the spectrum, here is a description of an excellent organization:

- All of the descriptors of an effective organization were presented.

- The sequencing of events built a compelling, even artistic expression of the idea, opinion, or argument being presented.

All aspects of a rubric should be focused on providing useful feedback to students that will help them to improve performance. As you develop the definitions of each scale item, it is also useful to develop recommendations that are appropriate for students when they achieve that particular rating. Returning to our organization element for the inadequate performance, the recommendations might include:

- Select a title after writing the objective, and make choices about content and organization.

- Rewrite the objective after a rough draft of the presentation.

- Use peer editing to get feedback concerning the sequence of storyboard elements.

- Rewrite the speaker notes in a way that effectively prompts the speaker to deliver a smooth performance.

Creating these recommendations up front will help provide students with consistent feedback based on the rubric definition.

Assessing Component Skills

No one doubts that domain knowledge is essential for transfer of problem solving within a domain. Unfortunately, too many people believe that domain knowledge can be adequately assessed by asking learners to recall what they know. Unfortunately, what we remember bears little relationship to what we understand. Domain knowledge should be about understanding how ideas in a domain are interconnected and, more important, how they affect each other. Domain knowledge should mean that students can apply their knowledge to solve problems. There are important cognitive activities or skills that are required in order to be able to solve problems. The two most important and readily assessable kinds are structural knowledge and causal reasoning.

Structural knowledge is the knowledge of how concepts within a domain are interrelated (Jonassen, Beissner, and Yacci, 1993). Concepts are understood not by memorizing definitions but by interrelating concepts with other domain concepts. They are interpreted as schemas that are defined by their interrelationships to other schemas. Explicitly describing those interrelationships is structural knowledge. Structural knowledge enables learners to form the complex interconnections required to make predictions and inferences necessary for solving problems. Structural knowledge refers to an individual's knowledge structure. *Knowledge structure* is the information-processing term for organized networks of information stored in semantic or long-term memory. It refers to the integration and organization of concepts in an individual's memory. Most important, structural knowledge is essential for problem solving.

A number of research studies have shown that knowledge structures are important in problem solving (Chi and Glaser, 1985). Robertson (1990) used think-aloud protocols to assess cognitive structure. He found that the extent to which those protocols contained relevant structural knowledge was a strong predictor of how well learners would solve transfer problems in physics on a written exam. In fact, structural knowledge was a much stronger predictor than either aptitude (as measured by standardized test scores) or performance on a set of similar problems. He concluded that cognitive structures that connect the formula and important concepts in the knowledge base are important to understanding physics principles—more important, it seems, than aptitude.

Structural knowledge can be assessed in many ways. In research, structural knowledge must first be elicited from the learners, usually in the form of word association lists or similarity ratings (Jonassen, Beissner, and Yacci, 1993). Structural knowledge is most easily elicited in word association lists. A free-association task presents students with an initial stimulus word and asks them to generate as many related words as they can think of within a specified time period (usually a minute). If students repeat this procedure with several domain concepts, it is possible to ascertain structural patterns among the words. Similarity ratings require students to perform a pairwise comparison of every concept on a list on a rating scale (for example, 1 = no relationship, 9 = means the same thing).

Following elicitation of the components of structural knowledge, it is necessary to represent the underlying structure among the concepts. This usually entails sophisticated statistics analysis, such as multidimensional scaling or cluster analysis, Pathfinder nets, or ordered and additive tree techniques. These analysis methods result in cognitive maps illustrating the student's knowledge structure (see Figure 8–2). Describing these methods is far beyond the scope of this chapter. (See Jonassen, Beissner, and Yacci, 1993, for more detail.)

Jonassen, Beissner, and Yacci (1993) describe a variety of verbal tests that can also be used. The simplest method of assessing the learner's comprehension of the relationships between concepts in the content domain is to ask the learner to describe or classify the conceptual nature of the relationships between important concepts. In order to assess the learner's understanding of

Figure 8–2. Pathfinder Net Showing a Student's Knowledge Structure.

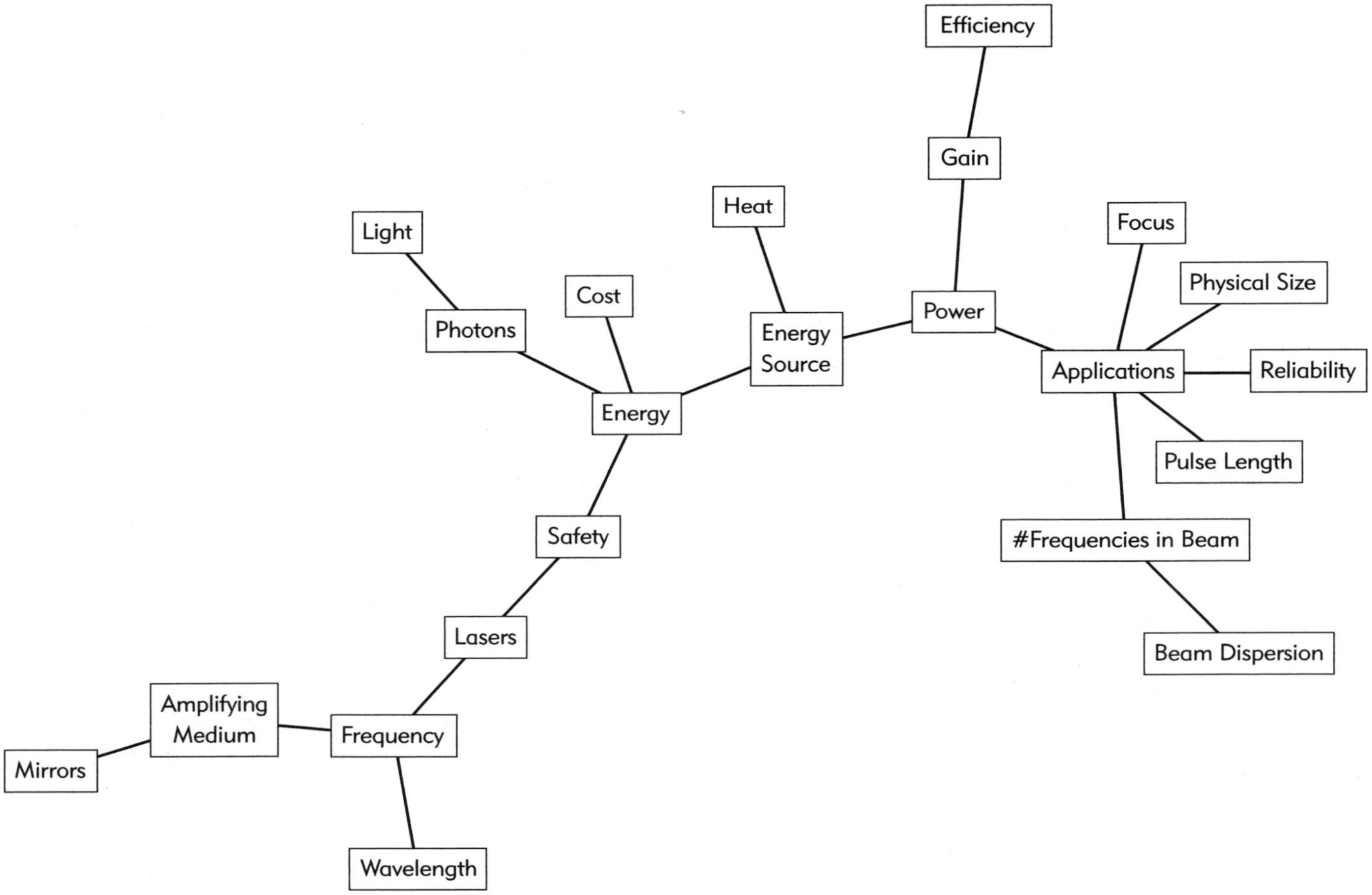

these relationships between concepts, ask the learner to classify the nature of the relationship between selected pairs of concepts. Although many possible links may be defined, most concepts are related in one of the following ways:

- has part/is part of
- has kind/is kind of
- causes/is caused by
- precedes/comes after
- describes (defines)/is description (definition) of
- assists/is assisted by
- has example/is example of
- justifies (rationalizes)/is justified (rationalized) by
- has characteristic/is characteristic of
- has opposite/is opposite of
- models/is modeled by

Notice that these categories describe relationships in both directions. They are asymmetric. That is, the relationship in one direction between concepts is different from the relationship in the other direction—for example, "Congress *has part* Senate" or "Senate *is part of* Congress." The relationship between two concepts may be directional or nondirectional. That is, you may state the relationship in one direction or both. Relationship tests can be effectively constructed using multiple-choice questions that present two concepts and ask students to select the best relationship—for example:

_____ Reinforcement . . . . ratios.

a. contains
b. is an instance of
c. is superordinate to
d. precedes

This type of question could also be presented in a short answer format:

capital _____ assets

Another method for assessing structural knowledge is analogies. Analogies describe two concepts and ask the learner to identify the relationship between those concepts and then to map that relationship on two other concepts. Typically this is accomplished by requiring the learner to select from a list of concepts the one that best fulfills the implied relationship in the first pair—for example:

Accounts receivable: assets:: _____ : liabilities

a. stock equity

b. loan income

c. accounts payable

d. goodwill

The essence of analogies is the transfer of knowledge from one situation to another by a process known as mapping, that is, finding aspects of correspondence between one set of concepts and another (Gick and Holyoak, 1983). Completing analogies requires well-integrated structural knowledge. Rather than merely describing the nature of the relationship between pairs of concepts, learners must map the structural similarities of one set of concepts onto another. Analogies are excellent descriptors of structural knowledge and predictors of problem solving, and they are easy to write.

Causal reasoning is the other important cognitive component skill related to problem solving. In Chapter Four, I described the process of causal reasoning and how it can be supported in learning environments. Causal reasoning, like structural knowledge, requires the attributions of one set of concepts to another. However, with causal reasoning, the attributions are causal. That is, one concept causes a change in state of another concept. Causal reasoning is perhaps the most important cognitive skill for problem solving, because problems usually involve changes in states brought on by causal factors. Assessing causal reasoning is most often accomplished by requiring students to make predictions or draw inferences about system components. A change in a chemical reagent will result in what kind of change in precipitate? These questions require that students apply structural knowledge while making predictions about the effects of one set on another. In order to assess causal reasoning, the questions must be scenario based; they must present a new, previously unencountered scenario to students that requires that students make a prediction about what will happen or draw an inference about what did happen.

Story Problems

In Chapter Two, I described the plight of Harvard physics professor Eric Mazur, who constructed tests to assess students' basic understanding of physics concepts represented in the problems that they solved so successfully. He did that because he found that many students had merely memorized equations and problem-solving procedures without understanding the concepts behind them, and he wanted them to understand the physics. In addition to assessing their ability to solve problems quantitatively, he also describes numerous conceptual questions in his book *Peer Instruction* (1997). Here is an example of a question that assesses structural knowledge:

Two marbles, one twice as heavy as the other, are dropped to the ground from the roof of a building. Just before hitting the ground, the heavier marble has

a. as much kinetic energy as the lighter one.
b. twice as much kinetic energy as the lighter one.
c. half as much kinetic energy as the lighter one.
d. four times as much kinetic energy as the lighter one.
e. The answer is impossible to determine.

Here is an example of a question that assesses causal reasoning:

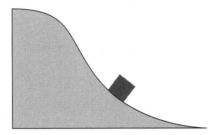

A cart on a roller coaster rolls down a track shown above. As the cart rolls beyond the point shown, what happens to its speed and acceleration in the direction of motion?

a. Both increase.

b. The speed decreases but the acceleration increases.

c. Both remain constant.

d. The speed increases but the acceleration decreases.

e. Both decrease.

Note that the task in both questions is not to solve a problem but rather to understand conceptual propositions and relationships well enough to make a prediction about mass and kinetic energy.

Another important kind of question that can be applied to story problems is a problem classification test. Present a new story problem to students and require the students to classify the kind of problem that it is. Rather than asking the student to solve the problem, a multiple-choice question would present a story problem and require the learner to identify the kind of problem—for example:

A skate boarder approaches a hill with a velocity of 3.5 m/s. The total mass of the board and the person is 80 kilograms. What is the kinetic energy of the board and rider? The skate board rider coasts up the hill. Assuming there is no friction, how high up the hill will the skate board coast?

> The problem is an example of which kind of physics problem?
>
> a. Newton's second law
> b. Conservation of energy
> c. Conservation of momentum
> d. Vectors

Problem classification tests are especially important in determining whether the student has constructed a model or schema for different kinds of problems. Being able to classify problem types is an essential skill in learning to solve story problems in different domains. It is a form of domain structural knowledge that enables students to distinguish between different kinds of problems and their particular solutions.

These structural knowledge, prediction, and inference questions assess the component cognitive skills required to solve physics story problems. Can these kinds of questions be used in place of performance assessments? They certainly can be, but especially with story problems, these kinds of questions assess a different set of cognitive skills from those required to solve the problem. It is best to assess students using both performance assessments and structural and causal reasoning questions.

Troubleshooting Problems

In Chapter Two, I argued that successful troubleshooting requires procedural knowledge, systemic (conceptual) knowledge, and strategic knowledge. All three kinds of knowledge require causal reasoning almost exclusively. In order to assess system knowledge of automotive electrical failures, you might use questions such as these:

> You are troubleshooting a car that will not start. You turn the ignition, and there is no response. The voltmeter shows that the battery is producing 13.6 volts. What is the most probable cause of the failure?

a. the ignition switch

b. the solenoid

c. the starter motor

d. the generator

The same situation could be used to assess strategic knowledge:

You are troubleshooting a car that will not start. You turn the ignition, and there is no response. The voltmeter shows that the battery is producing 13.6 volts. The next test that you should conduct is

a. voltage to the ignition.

b. voltage to the starter.

c. amperage to the starter.

d. amperage from the battery.

Understanding a domain (systems knowledge) also entails knowing how the system is organized or constructed. Structural knowledge questions can assess systems knowledge of the students—for example:

The voltage travels most directly from the battery to the

a. solenoid.

b. ignition switch.

c. starter.

d. generator.

Recalling system configurations is necessary for diagnosing faults, but it is not sufficient. Learners must apply what they remember to making predictions, drawing inferences, or explaining changes in system states, that is, answering causal reasoning questions. Therefore, it is necessary to create a new scenario that was not used during instruction to assess this kind of causal reasoning. Without both kinds of knowledge, students will not be able to learn to troubleshoot problems.

Case Analysis Problems

Case analysis problems are similar to story problems and troubleshooting problems in that they require that learners develop causal reasoning about the problem domain. The primary difference between case analysis problems and the others is their complexity. There are usually far more factors with less predictability and more interactions, so the amount of conceptual knowledge required to solve problems is much greater than for story problems.

The water pollution problem described earlier in this chapter would require numerous questions to assess structural knowledge and causal reasoning. You would want to be able to predict the growth of antigens based on environmental conditions. Why different antigens are found in different environments? And you would need to predict physiological effects of different antigens under different conditions. What are the effects of different chemical or physical actions on the growth of antigens? There are a host of other political, social, and economic conditions that will also predict the ability of any country to deal with water-borne illnesses. There are literally hundreds of questions that could be asked about the water-borne illnesses in order to assess learners' causal reasoning and domain knowledge.

Knowledge Representation Tools

It is not always necessary to ask questions or give examinations in order to assess knowledge or skills. In Chapter Four, I described different tools for representing problems, including semantic networking, expert systems, influence diagrams, and systems models. In the context of that chapter, the purpose for using those tools was to help learners to construct models of the problem space in order to understand the problem better. However, the models that students build can also be used to assess their domain knowledge. In many ways, they are better assessments of domain knowledge than individual questions because they show students' understanding of the interconnectedness of the components in a knowledge domain. Do not be afraid to substitute them for examinations.

If you use the models that students construct as assessments, you will need to construct rubrics for assessing their models. Those rubrics should address the quality of the models themselves. Examples of rubrics for assessing expert systems constructed by students are shown in Exhibit 8–5.

Exhibit 8–5. Example Rubrics for Assessing Expert Systems Constructed by Students.

System factors accurately describe system

Simulates coherent thinking; models meaningful activity	Consistently simulates thinking; anomalies occur	Inconsistently represents thinking	Simulates implausible or inaccurate thinking; poorly models activity; represents associative thinking

Advice is complete and accurate

Advice is always plausible; explains reasoning, enhances user understanding	Advice is useful but missing a few important elements; misses some reasoning	Advice is inconsistent; misses important elements or conclusions	Provides vague, implausible advice with no explanations or reasoning; does not enhance understanding

Consistency of advice

Accurately predicts/infers/ explains correct values always	Occasionally provides no advice but usually predicts or infers appropriate advice	Frequently provides no advice; often fails to provide appropriate advice	Running system often results in no advice; combinations not anticipated; insufficient rules or rule combinations

In addition to these rubrics, content or domain-specific rubrics need to be used to assess the quality of domain understanding. While writing rubrics to assess these models may be more difficult, the benefits of model building should justify the effort. Additionally, assessing the models will convey their importance to the students. Students know that what is important is what gets assessed and used to determine their grades. If model construction is graded, it will be accorded more importance and effort.

Assessing Argumentation and Justification

Because argumentation is an implied component in every kind of problem solving (see Chapter Six), students' argumentation about how and why they solved problems as they did can be an important form of assessment when judging the quality of problem solving. If students can argue effectively about their solutions to problems, how they solved the problem, or why they did what they did, they provide additional confirmatory evidence about their problem-solving ability. Therefore, I briefly examine argumentation as a third kind of assessment that can be used to assess problem solving. It is best to use argumentation in combination with performance assessments and assessments of constituent cognitive skills.

Student arguments can be collected using a variety of methods. Argumentation can be measured using objective forms of measurement such as multiple-choice questions. Student arguments can also be assessed by using verbal protocol analysis (described before), argumentation codes to classify messages generated during discussion, or student think-aloud processes.

Objective Forms of Assessment of Argumentation

Argumentation skills can be assessed using objective forms of assessment, such as multiple-choice tests. Questions requiring argumentative reasoning can form the stem of a test item—for example:

Which warrant best supports the claim that Candidate X should become the next president of the United States?

a. Candidate X is favored in most polls taken last week.
b. Candidate Y believes that she should be the next president.
c. Candidate X has more money in campaign contributions.
d. Candidate X has more advertisements on television.

Students who work harder in school will make a better living after school. Which is the most appropriate assumption on which this premise and conclusion are based?

a. Attitude is the most important difference; those who work harder get more.
b. What your teachers think of you is the strongest predictor of success.
c. Skills acquired in school better prepare you to function in the real world.
d. The harder you work, the more you know.

The stock market has fallen 200 points in the last week. Which conclusion logically follows from that premise?

a. Buy more stock; it's a bargain.
b. Sell all of my stock; the economy is broken.
c. The economy is inflationary.
d. Consumer confidence is down.

These questions can also be developed to specifically assess the arguments required to solve a particular kind of problem. There is no research on the use of this form of assessment and its relationship to problem solving. Although this form of assessment is easy, it probably will not provide sufficient evidence of problem-solving ability to be used alone.

Coding Student Arguments

When students are engaged in an argumentative discussion, either face-to-face or on-line, their arguments can also be assessed. If the discussion is face-to-face, it is necessary to transcribe the discussion in order to assess it later. When assessing on-line discussions, most bulletin board software allows you to save each student message as a separate record in a database. The messages that students posted that are stored in the database can be counted and qualitatively analyzed for which components of argumentation are present in each posting.

Cho and Jonassen (2002) analyzed student on-line discussion while solving problems by using a coding scheme adapted from Toulmin's model of argument. The model (Toulmin, Rieke, and Janik, 1984) identifies five major components of argument: claims, grounds, warrants, backings, and rebuttals. Each message was classified by two coders into one of those five categories without knowing the identity of the group. After classifying all of the messages, we counted the number of each category used during the discussion. Analysis showed that students using an argumentation scaffold, Belvedere (described in Chapter Six), produced significantly more argument components during group discussions than did subjects in the discussion groups that did not have access to the scaffold. Specifically, groups using the scaffold produced significantly more claims and grounds than groups that did not have access to the scaffold. The analysis also showed that groups solving ill-structured problems produced more arguments during group discussions than students solving well-structured problems, especially in stating rebuttals. Groups solving ill-structured tasks produced more rebuttals than those solving well-structured problems because this kind of reasoning is more important to that kind of problem solving.

Protocol analysis can also be used to assess individual student contributions during a group discussion. By sorting the database by student, individual contributions for each student can be summed, compared, and evaluated. The number of claims, grounds, and warrants contributed by each individual provides an important measure of his or her contribution to the group discussion and problem solving.

In Chapter Six, I described a scaffolded discussion board that requires students to classify the kind of argumentation they were using before posting the message. That system outputs a database of each student's comments with their classification, date, and time. What makes that system powerful is that it also continuously provides information about the structure of the discussion. The moderator always knows the percentages and ratios of claims to warrants to evidence. The moderator also knows the percentages of each kind of warrant and evidence used. My experience with the scaffolded discussion board has shown me that students almost always support each other; they seldom refute each other's claims. With one class, I also noticed immediately that the only kinds of evidence that students used were "personal beliefs" or "personal experiences." For purposes of assessment, this information would result in failing grades. For purposes of moderating, it provided me the opportunity to perturb the students' arguments by suggesting that the credibility of their evidence was very questionable and all too consistent. In order to support their claim or conclusions, they had to use other sources of evidence.

Assessing Student Essays and Problem-Solving Accounts

Verbal protocol analysis can be used to assess argumentation in individual students' essays. When students are individually assigned to solve problems similar to those they have learned to solve and describe their solution, they write an individual essay to describe how they would solve the problem, what their solutions were, and why they used the problem-solving approach that they did. Halpern (2003) describes a process for analyzing student essays that includes the following steps:

1. Parse the text. Determine if it contains an argument. Are there at least one premise and one conclusion? If not, you are done.

2. Identify all of the stated and unstated components, including premises, conclusions, assumptions, and counterarguments.

3. Assess the acceptability of the premises. If the premises are unfounded, you are done. If they are acceptable, then determine

whether the premises are inconsistent with each other. If only some are unacceptable, then eliminate them.

4. Diagram the argument. Rate the strength of the support as nonexistent, weak, medium, or strong. Do the premises provide consistent support?

5. Assess the strength of the counterarguments and assumptions. Do they compromise the support provided by the premises?

6. Make an overall evaluation of the soundness of the argument. Is it unsound, strong, or somewhere in between?

This method requires reading and evaluating students' argumentative essays. It is based on the strength of relationships between premises, conclusions, assumptions, and counterarguments articulated by Halpern (2003). Norris and Ennis (1989) suggested the following criteria for evaluating argumentative essays:

- Do you clearly state the conclusion and define the necessary terms?

- Are the materials that you included relevant to the conclusion?

- Is the argument sound? Do the premises support the conclusion?

- Have you considered the credibility of your experts?

- Is the essay well organized, with each argument laid out separately?

- Have you fairly represented opposing points of view and counterarguments?

- Have you used good grammar and a clear style of writing?

In Exhibit 8–6, I synthesize a series of assessment rubrics for assessing the quality of students' argumentative reports or essays based on Halpern's conception of arguments. When students construct arguments as part of the problem solution or as an addendum to their solutions, use these rubrics to assess the quality of their arguments.

Exhibit 8–6. Example Rubrics for Assessing Argumentative Work.

Quality of conclusions (claims)

Conclusions unrelated to problem needs or solution	Few conclusions relate to problem needs or solutions; inconsistent relationships	Conclusions relate to problem generally, but some unclear; usually support stated solution	All conclusions relevant to problem; support solutions; related to needs

Premises are sound

Premises not related to conclusions	Relationship of premises to conclusions is inconsistent; not related well with other premises	Most premises support conclusion	All premises support specific conclusion; add strength to the conclusion; consistent with other premises

Adequacy of premises

No premises stated; only unsupported conclusions	Few premises stated; most unclear	Most premises stated explicitly; most clear	All premises stated explicitly and clearly

Assumptions related

Completely unstated and unknown	Few stated but not associated with premises or conclusions; mostly unreasonable or invalid	Most assumptions stated; not all connected to conclusions or premises; some invalid	Clearly stated; consistent with claims and premises; reasonable and valid

Exhibit 8–6. Example Rubrics for Assessing Argumentative Work, Cont'd.

Credibility of premises

Sources of evidence are weak, filled with unsupportable evidence and propaganda	Sources of evidence are questionable or origin is unknown	Sources of evidence mostly valid with limited amounts of unknown data	Sources of evidence (personal, written) are unimpeachable; accepted as fact

Counterarguments accommodated

No counterarguments acknowledged	Only one or two counterarguments acknowledged; none argued or rejected	Most counterarguments addressed; refutation not premise-based	All counterarguments identified and refuted using valid, supportable premises

Organization of arguments

Arguments are indistinguishable; unorganized; do not support each other	Arguments identified; relationships to each other not obvious	Arguments articulated but partially integrated; relationships to each other usually positive	Each argument separated; sequenced logically to support solution to problem

Student essays or individual verbal or written accounts of problem solving may also be assessed using rubrics based on Toulmin's conception of argumentation, which focuses on claims, supported by warrants, supported by backing or evidence (see Exhibit 8–7). Cho and Jonassen (2002) scored individual reports of how problems were solved using the scoring rubric in Exhibit 8–7 in order to determine the quality of argumentation based on Toulmin's model of argument (Toulmin, Rieke, and Janik, 1984). Individual scores were achieved by summing the number of points achieved in each argumentation category (claims, grounds, warrants, backings, and rebuttal).

Exhibit 8–7. **Example Rubrics Based on Claims, Grounds, Warrants, Backings,**
       and Rebuttals.

Claims

No claim related to the proposition or unclear assertions	The writer makes generalizations that are related to the proposition, but the assertions lack specificity or offer unclear referents. The writer leaves much for the reader to infer in order to determine the impact of the claim.	The writer states generalizations that are related to the propositions, but the assertions are not complete. Enough information is available to figure out the writer's intent, but much is left to the reader to determine.	The writer states generalizations that are related to the proposition and are clear and complete.

Grounds

No supporting data offered or the data are not related to the claim	The data or evidence are weak, inaccurate, or incomplete—for example, an attempt at using a general principle without establishing the truth of the principle; the use of examples from personal experience which are not generalizable; the citation of data when no source is identified; or the use of obviously biased or outdated material.	The data offered are relevant but not complete. The writer leaves much for the reader to infer from the data. The writer may have offered the data without the complete citation, which would allow the reader to determine the reliability of the data as evidence. The writer may offer data that are not complete enough to allow the reader to determine their significance.	The supporting data are compete, accurate, and relevant to the claim.

Exhibit 8–7. Example Rubrics Based on Claims, Grounds, Warrants, Backings, and Rebuttals, Cont'd.

Warrants

No rules and principles offered	The writer recognizes a need to connect the data to the claim and states some elaboration of data, but the writer fails to make the connection, or most rules and principles are not valid or relevant.	The writer explains the data in some way, but the explanation is not linked specifically to the claim.	The writer explains the data in such a way that it is clear how they support the claim.

Backings

No sources of warrants given	The writer states incorrect, irrelevant sources of warrants.	The writer states correct, relevant sources of warrants but the sources are very general, not specific.	The writer states correct, relevant, and specific sources of warrants.

Rebuttals

No recognition of constraints of solutions	The writer offers a few constraints of solutions, but the constraints are not elaborated.	The writer identifies constraints of solutions, but the constraints are not sufficient.	The writer states complete and systematic identification of constraints of solutions.

SUMMARY

In this chapter, I have described three important methods for assessing students' problem-solving abilities: performance assessment, component skills, and argumentation. These are not the only methods for assessing problem solving. There is potentially an endless combination of options. However, I believe that these are the most predictive and descriptive of students' abilities to solve problems. Together, they paint a more complete picture of students' understanding, skills, and performance. Problem solving requires all three. These methods should be used in combination with each other, not in isolation.

REFERENCES

Alessi, S. "Building vs. Using Simulations." In J. M. Spector and T. M. Anderson (eds.), *Integrated and Holistic Perspectives on Learning, Instruction, and Technology.* Norwell, Mass.: Kluwer, 2000.

Anderson, J. R. *Cognitive Psychology and Its Implications.* New York: Freeman, 1980.

Anderson, J. R. *The Architecture of Cognition.* Cambridge, Mass.: Harvard University Press, 1983.

Anzai, Y. "Learning and Use of Representations for Physics Problems." In K. A. Ericsson and J. Smith (eds.), *Toward a General Theory of Expertise.* Cambridge: Cambridge University Press, 1991.

Asher, H. B. *Causal Modeling.* Beverly Hills, Calif.: Sage, 1983.

Atkinson, R., Derry, S. J., Renkl, A., and Wortham, D. "Learning from Examples: Instructional Principles from the Worked Examples Research." *Review of Educational Research, 70,* 2000, 181–215.

Atman, C. J., and Bursic, K. M. "Documenting a Process: The Use of Verbal Protocol Analysis to Study Engineering Student Design." *Journal of Engineering Education,* 1998, Special Issue, 121–132.

Atman, C. J., and Turns, J. "Studying Engineering Design Learning: Four Verbal Protocol Studies." In C. Eastman, M. McCracken, and W. Newstetter (eds.), *Knowing and Learning to Design: Cognitive Perspectives in Design Education.* New York: Elsevier, 2001.

Bagno, E., Eylon, B. S., and Ganiel, U. "From Fragmented Knowledge to a Knowledge Structure: Linking the Domains of Mechanics and Electromagnetism." *American Journal of Physics, Supplement,* 2000, *68*(7), S16-S26.

Bardach, E. *A Practical Guide for Policy Analysis: The Eightfold Path to More Effective Problem Solving.* New York: Chatham, 2000.

Baxter-Magolda, M. B. "Comparing Open-Ended Interviews and Standardized Measures of Intellectual Development." *Journal of College Student Personnel,* 1987, *28,* 443–448.

Bell, P., and Linn, M. "Scientific Arguments as Learning Artifacts: Designing for Learning on the Web in KIE." *International Journal of Science Education,* 2000, *22*(8), 797–817.

Blake, R. L., Hosokawa, M. C., and Riley, S. L. "Student Performances on Step 1 and Step 2 of the United States Medical Licensing Examination Following Implementation of a Problem-Based Learning Curriculum." *Academic Medicine,* 2000, *75,* 66–70.

Blessing, S. B., and Ross, B. H. "Content Effects in Problem Categorization and Problem Solving." *Journal of Experimental Psychology: Learning, Memory, and Cognition,* 1996, *22*(3), 792–810.

Bransford, J., and Stein, B. S. *The IDEAL Problem Solver: A Guide for Improving Thinking, Learning, and Creativity.* New York: Freeman, 1993.

Briars, D. J., and Larkin, J. H. "An Integrated Model of Skill in Solving Elementary Word Problems." *Cognition and Instruction,* 1984, *1,* 245–296.

Brown, S. I., and Walter, M. I. *The Art of Problem Posing.* (2nd ed.) Mahwah, N.J.: Erlbaum, 1990.

Bruner, J. *Acts of Meaning.* Cambridge, Mass.: Harvard University Press, 1990.

Carter, K. "What Is a Case? What Is Not a Case?" In M. A. Lundeberg, B. B. Levin, and H. L. Harrington (eds.), *Who Learns What from Cases and How: The Research Base for Teaching and Learning with Cases.* Mahwah, N.J.: Erlbaum, 1999.

Catrambone, R. "Improving Examples to Improve Transfer to Novel Problems." *Memory and Cognition,* 1994, *22*(5), 606–615.

Catrambone, R. "Generalizing Solution Procedures Learned from Examples." *Journal of Experimental Psychology: Learning, Memory, and Cognition,* 1996, *22*(4), 1020–1031.

Cerbin, B. *The Nature and Development of Informal Reasoning Skills in College Students,* 1988. (ED 298 805)

Chi, M.T.H., and Bassock, M. "Learning from Examples vs. Self-Explanations." In L. B. Resnick (ed.), *Knowing, Learning, and Instruction: Essays in Honor of Robert Glaser.* Mahwah, N.J.: Erlbaum, 1989.

Chi, M.T.H., Feltovich, P. J., and Glaser, R. "Categorization and Representation of Physics Problems by Experts and Novices." *Cognitive Science,* 1981, *5,* 12–152.

Chi, M.T.H., and Glaser, R. "Problem Solving Ability." In R. S. Sternberg (ed.), *Human Abilities: An Information Processing Approach.* New York: Freeman, 1985.

Chi, M.T.H., and others. "Self-Explanations: How Students Study and Use Examples in Learning to Solve Problems." *Cognitive Science,* 1989, *13,* 145–182.

Chi, M.T.H., and VanLehn, K. A. "The Content of Physics Self-Explanations." *Journal of the Learning Sciences,* 1991, *1*(1), 69–105.

Cho, K. L., and Jonassen, D. H. "The Effects of Argumentation Scaffolds on Argumentation and Problem Solving." *Educational Technology: Research and Development,* 2002, *50* (3), 5–22.

Churchman, C. W. *The Design of Inquiring Systems: Basic Concepts of Systems and Organizations.* New York: Basic Books, 1971.

Cognition and Technology Group at Vanderbilt. "The Jasper Experiment: An Exploration of Issues in Learning and Instructional Design." *Educational Technology: Research and Development,* 1992, *40*(1), 65–80.

Console, L., and Torasso, P. "Hypothetical Reasoning in Causal Models." *International Journal of Intelligent Systems,* 1990, *5,* 83–124.

Cooper, G., and Sweller, J. "Effects of Schema Acquisition and Rule Automation on Mathematical Problem Solving." *Journal of Educational Psychology,* 1987, *79,* 347–362.

Coulson, R. L., Feltovich, P. J., and Spiro, R. J. "Foundations of a Misunderstanding of the Ultrastructural Basis of Myocardial Failure: A Reciprocation Network of Oversimplifications." *Journal of Medicine and Philosophy,* 1989, *14,* 109–146.

de Jong, T., and Ferguson-Hessler, M.G.M. "Knowledge of Problem Situations in Physics: A Comparison of Good and Poor Novice Problem Solvers." *Learning and Instruction,* 1991, *1,* 289–302.

de Jong, T., and van Joolingen, W. R. "Scientific Discovery Learning with Computers: Simulations of Conceptual Domains." *Review of Educational Research,* 1998, *68*(2), 179–201.

De Kleer, J., and Brown, J. S. "Mental Models of Physical Mechanisms and Their Acquisition." In J. R. Anderson (ed.), *Cognitive Skills and Their Acquisition.* Mahwah, N.J.: Erlbaum, 1981.

Derry, S. J., and the TiPS Research Group. *Development and Assessment of Tutorials in Problem Solving (TiPS): A Remedial Mathematics Tutor.* Madison: Wisconsin Center for Education Research, University of Wisconsin-Madison, 2001.

Devi, R., Tiberghien, A., Baker, M., and Brna, P. "Modeling Students' Construction of Energy Modes in Physics." *Instructional Science,* 1996, *24,* 259–293.

Dörner, D., and Wearing, A. J. "Complex Problem Solving: Toward a Theory." In P. A. Frensch and J. Funke (eds.), *Complex Problem Solving: The European Perspective.* Mahwah, N.J.: Erlbaum, 1995.

Dunkle, M. E., Schraw, G., and Bendixen, L. D. "Cognitive Processes in Well-Defined and Ill-Defined Problem Solving." Paper presented at the annual meeting of the American Educational Research Association, San Francisco, Apr. 1995.

Elliott, S. N. *Creating Meaningful Performance Assessments.* [http://www.ed.gov/databases/ERIC_Digests/ed381985.html]. 1995. (ED 381 985)

English, L. D. "Children's Reasoning in Solving Relational Problems of Deduction." *Thinking and Reasoning,* 1998, *4*(3), 249–281.

Ericsson, K. A., and Simon, H. A. *Protocol Analysis: Verbal Reports, as Data.* Cambridge, Mass.: MIT Press, 1993.

Feltovich, P. J., Spiro, R. J., and Coulson, R. L. "The Nature of Conceptual Understanding in Biomedicine: The Deep Structure of Complex Ideas and the Development of Misconceptions." In D. Evans and V. Patel (eds.), *The Cognitive Sciences in Medicine.* Cambridge, Mass.: MIT Press, 1989.

Fishbein, D. D., and others. "Learners' Questions and Comprehension in a Tutoring System." *Journal of Educational Psychology,* 1990, *82,* 163–170.

Funke, J. "Solving Complex Problems: Exploration and Control of Complex Systems." In R. J. Sternberg and P. A. Frensch (eds.), *Complex Problem Solving: Principles and Mechanisms.* Mahwah, N.J.: Erlbaum, 1991.

Gagné, R. M. *Conditions of Learning.* New York: Holt, Rinehart, and Winston, 1960.

Gick, M. L. "Problem-Solving Strategies." *Educational Psychologist,* 1986, *21*(1–2), 99–120.

Gick, M. L., and Holyoak, K. J. "Schema Induction and Analogical Transfer." *Cognitive Psychology,* 1983, *15,* 1–38.

Grabinger, R. S., Wilson, B. G., and Jonassen, D. H. *Designing Expert Systems for Education.* Westport, Conn.: Praeger, 1990.

Greeno, J. G. "Understanding and Procedural Knowledge in Mathematics Instruction." *Educational Psychologist, 12*(3), 1978, 262–283.

Halpern, D. F. *Thought and Knowledge: An Introduction to Critical Thinking.* (4th ed.) Mahwah, N.J.: Erlbaum, 2003.

Hanna, J. "Learning Environment Criteria." In R. Ennals, R. Gwyn, and L. Zdravcher (eds.), *Information Technology and Education: The Changing School.* Columbus, OH: Ellis Horwood, 1986.

Hastie, R. "Causes and Effects of Causal Attribution." *Journal of Personality and Social Psychology,* 1984, *46,* 44–56.

Henning, P. H. "A Qualitative Study of Situated Learning by Refrigeration Service Technicians Working for a Supermarket Chain in Northeastern Pennsylvania." Unpublished doctoral dissertation, Pennsylvania State University, 1996.

Hernandez-Serrano, J., and Jonassen, D. H. "The Effects of Case Libraries on Problem Solving." *Journal of Computer-Assisted Learning,* 2003, *19,* 103–114.

Hong, N. S., Jonassen, D. H., and McGee, S. "Predictors of Well-Structured and Ill-Structured Problem Solving in an Astronomy Simulation." *Journal of Research in Science Teaching,* 2003, *40*(1), 6–33.

Jaspers, J.M.F. "Mental Models of Causal Reasoning." In D. Bar-Tal and A. W. Kruglanski (eds.), *The Social Psychology of Knowledge.* Cambridge: Cambridge University Press, 1988.

Johnson, M. "Facilitating High Quality Student Practice in Introductory Physics." *American Journal of Physics Supplement,* 2001, *69*(7), S2-S11.

Johnson, S. D. "Cognitive Analysis of Expert and Novice Trouble-shooting Performance." *Performance Improvement Quarterly,* 1988, *1*(3), 38–54.

Jonassen, D. H. "Instructional Design Model for Well-Structured and Ill-Structured Problem-Solving Learning Outcomes." *Educational Technology: Research and Development,* 1997, *45*(1), 65–95.

Jonassen, D. H. "Toward a Design Theory of Problem Solving." *Educational Technology: Research and Development,* 2000a, *48*(4), 63–85.

Jonassen, D. H. *Computers as Mindtools for Schools: Engaging Critical Thinking.* Upper Saddle River, N.J.: Prentice-Hall, 2000b.

Jonassen, D. H. "Revisiting Activity Theory as a Framework for Designing Student-Centered Learning Environments." In D. H. Jonassen and S. M. Land (eds.), *Theoretical Foundations of Learning Environments.* Mahwah, N.J.: Erlbaum, 2000c.

Jonassen, D. H. "Learning as Activity." *Educational Technology,* 2002, *42*(2), 45–51.

Jonassen, D. H. "Designing Research-Based Instruction for Story Problems." *Educational Psychology Review,* 2003, *15*(3), 267–296.

Jonassen, D. H., Ambruso, D. R., and Olesen, J. "Designing a Hypertext on Transfusion Medicine Using Cognitive Flexibility Theory." *Journal of Educational Hypermedia and Multimedia,* 1992, *1*(3), 309–322.

Jonassen, D. H., Beissner, K., and Yacci, M. *Structural Knowledge: Techniques for Assessing, Conveying, and Acquiring Structural Knowledge.* Mahwah, N.J.: Erlbaum, 1993.

Jonassen, D. H., and Henning, P. "Mental Models: Knowledge in the Head and Knowledge in the World." *Educational Technology,* 1999, *39*(3), 37–42.

Jonassen, D. H., and Hernandez-Serrano, J. "Case-Based Reasoning and Instructional Design: Using Stories to Support Problem Solving." *Educational Technology: Research and Development,* 2002, *50*(2), 65–77.

Jonassen, D. H., Howland, J., Moore, J. and Marra, R. M. *Learning to Solve Problems with Technology: A Constructivist Perspective.* Columbus, Ohio: Merrill/Prentice-Hall, 2003.

Jonassen, D. H., and Kwon, H. I. "Communication Patterns in Computer-Mediated vs. Face-to-Face Group Problem Solving." *Educational Technology: Research and Development,* 2001, *49*(10), 35–52.

Jonassen, D. H., Mann, E., and Ambruso, D. J. "Causal Modeling for Structuring Case-Based Learning Environments." *Intelligent Tutoring Media,* 1996, *6*(3/4), 103–112.

Jonassen, D. H., Marra, R. M., and Palmer, B. "Epistemological Development: An Implicit Entailment of Constructivist Learning Environments." In S. Dijkstra and N. Seel (eds.), *Instructional Design: International Perspectives.* Mahwah, N.J.: Erlbaum, 2004.

Jonassen, D. H., Prevish, T., Christy, D., and Stavurlaki, E. "Learning to Solve Problems on the Web: Aggregate Planning in a Business Management Course." *Distance Education: An International Journal,* 1999, *20*(1), 49–63.

Jones, D. R., and Schkade, D. A. "Choosing and Translating Between Problem Representations." *Organizational Behavior and Human Decision Processes,* 1995, *61*(2), 214–223.

Kelly, H. H. "The Process of Causal Attribution." *American Psychologist,* 1973, *28,* 107–128.

Kitchner, K. S. "Cognition, Metacognition, and Epistemic Cognition: A Three-Level Model of Cognitive Processing." *Human Development,* 1983, *26,* 222–232.

Kitchner, K. S., and King, P. M. "Reflective Judgment: Concepts of Justification and Their Relationship to Age and Education." *Journal of Applied Developmental Psychology,* 1981, *2,* 89–116.

Klein, G. A., and Calderwood, R. "How Do People Use Analogs to Make Decisions?" In J. Kolodner (ed.), *Proceedings: Workshop on Case-Based Reasoning (DARPA).* San Mateo, Calif.: Morgan Kaufmann, 1988.

Kluwe, R. H. "Single Case Studies and Models of Complex Problem Solving." In P. A. Frensch and J. Funke (eds.), *Complex Problem Solving: The European Perspective.* Mahwah, N.J.: Erlbaum, 1995.

Knudson, R. E. "Effects of Instructional Strategies, Grade and Sex on Students' Persuasive Writing." *Journal of Experimental Education,* 1991, *59*(2), 141–152.

Kolodner, J. *Case-Based Reasoning.* San Mateo, Calif.: Morgan Kaufmann, 1993.

Kolodner, J. L., Hmelo, C. E., and Narayanan, N. H. "Problem-Based Learning Meets Case-Based Reasoning." In D. C. Edelson and E. A. Domeshek (eds.), *Proceedings of the International Conference on the Learning Sciences.* Evanston, Ill.: Northwestern University, 1996.

Kopeikina, L., Brandau, R., and Lemmon, A. "Case-Based Reasoning for Continuous Control." In J. Kolodner (ed.), *Proceedings: Workshop on Case-Based Reasoning (DARPA).* San Mateo, Calif.: Morgan Kaufmann, 1988.

Koslowski, B., Okagaki, L., Lorenz, C., and Umbach, D. "When Covariation Is Not Enough: The Role of Causal Mechanism, Sampling Method, and Sample Size in Causal Reasoning." *Child Development, 60,* 1989, 1316–1327.

Kuhn, D. *The Skills of Argument.* Cambridge: Cambridge University Press, 1991.

Kuhn, D. "Thinking as Argument." *Harvard Education Review,* 1992, *62* (2), 155–178.

Lancaster, J. S., and Kolodner, J. L. "Problem Solving in a Natural Task as a Function of Experience." In *Proceedings of the Ninth Annual Conference of the Cognitive Science Society.* Mahwah, N.J.: Erlbaum, 1988.

Larkin, J. H. "The Role of Problem Representation in Physics." In D. Gentner and A. L. Stevens (eds.), *Mental Models.* Mahwah, N.J.: Erlbaum, 1983.

Lave, J. *Cognition in Practice: Mind, Mathematics, and Everyday Life.* Cambridge: Cambridge University Press, 1988.

Lehman, D., Lempert, R., and Nisbett, R. E. "The Effects of Graduate Training on Reasoning: Formal Discipline and Thinking About Everyday-Life Events." *Educational Psychologist,* 1988, *43,* 431–442.

Lester, J. C., Stone, B. A., and Stelling, G. D. "Lifelike Pedagogical Agents for Mixed-Initiative Problem Solving in Constructivist Learning Environments." *User Modeling and User-Adapted Interaction,* 1999, *9,* 1–44.

Lindeman, B., and others. "Exploring Cases Online with Virtual Environments." In J. L. Schnase and E. L. Cunnius (eds.), *Proceedings of the First International Conference on Computer-Supported Collaborative Learning.* Mahwah, N.J.: Erlbaum, 1995.

Lochhead, J. *Thinkback: A User's Guide to Minding the Mind.* Mahwah, N.J.: Erlbaum, 2001.

Lucangelli, D., Tressoldi, P. E., and Cendron, M. "Cognitive and Metacognitive Abilities Involved in the Solution of Mathematical Word Problems: Validation of a Comprehensive Model." *Contemporary Educational Psychology,* 1998, *23,* 257–275.

Lundeberg, M. A. "Discovering Teaching and Learning Through Cases." In M. A. Lundeberg, B. B. Levin, and H. L. Harrington (eds.), *Who Learns What from Cases and How: The Research Base for Teaching and Learning with Cases.* Mahwah, N.J.: Erlbaum, 1999.

Marshall, S. P. *Schemas in Problem Solving.* Cambridge: Cambridge University Press, 1995.

Marttunen, M. "Assessing Argumentation Skills Among Finnish University Students." *Learning and Instruction,* 1994, *4,* 175–191.

Mayer, R. E. "Comprehension as Affected by Structure of Problem Representation." *Memory and Cognition,* 1976, *4*(3), 249–255.

Mayer, R. E. "Memory for Algebra Story Problems." *Journal of Educational Psychology,* 1982, *74,* 199–216.

Mayer, R. E. *Thinking, Problem Solving, Cognition.* (2nd ed.) New York: Freeman, 1992.

Mayer, R. E., Larkin, J. H., Kadane, J. B. "A Cognitive Analysis of Mathematical Problem Solving Ability." In R. Sternberg (ed.), *Advances in the Psychology of Human Intelligence.* Mahwah, N.J.: Erlbaum, 1984.

Mazur, E. *Peer Instruction: A User's Manual.* Upper Saddle River, N.J.: Prentice Hall, 1997.

McEwan, H., and Egan, K. *Narrative in Teaching, Learning, and Research.* New York: Teachers College Press, 1995.

Moore, D. "A Framework for Using Multimedia Within Argumentation Systems." *Journal of Educational Multimedia and Hypermedia,* 2000, *9*(2), 83–98.

Moore, E. A., and Agogino, A. M. "INFORM: An Architecture for Expert Directed Knowledge Acquisition." *International Journal of Man-Machine Studies,* 1987, *26,* 213–230.

Mwangi, W., and Sweller, J. "Learning to Solve Compare Word Problems: The Effect of Example Format for Generating Self-Explanations." *Cognition and Instruction,* 1998, *16,* 173–199.

Nathan, M. J. "Knowledge and Situational Feedback in a Learning Environment for Algebra Story Problem Solving." *Interactive Learning Environments,* 1998, *5,* 135–139.

Nathan M. J., Kintsch, W., and Young, E. "A Theory of Algebra-Word-Problem Comprehension and Its Implications for the Design of Learning Environments." *Cognition and Instruction,* 1992, *9,* 329–389.

Newell, A., and Simon, H. *Human Problem Solving.* Upper Saddle River, N.J.: Prentice Hall, 1972.

Nisbett, R., and Ross, L. *Human Inference: Strategies and Shortcoming of Social Judgment.* Upper Saddle River, N.J.: Prentice Hall, 1980.

Norris, S. P., and Ennis, R. H. *Evaluating Critical Thinking.* Pacific Grove, Calif.: Critical Thinking Press, 1989.

Novak, G. M., Patterson, E. T., Gavrin, A. D., and Christianson, W. *Just-in-Time Teaching: Blending Active Learning with Web Technology.* Upper Saddle River, N.J.: Prentice Hall, 1999.

Novick, L. R. "Analogical Transfer, Problem Similarity, and Expertise." *Journal of Experimental Psychology,* 1988, *14,* 510–520.

Orr, J. E. *Talking About Machines: An Ethnography of a Modern Job.* Ithaca, N.Y.: Cornell University Press, 1996.

Panitz, B. "The Fifteen-Minute Lecture." *Prism,* Nov. 1998, p. 17.

Perkins, D. N., and Grotzer, T. A. "Models and Modes: Focusing on Dimensions of Causal Complexity to Achieve Deeper Scientific Understanding." Paper presented at the annual meeting of the American Educational Research Association, New Orleans, La., Apr. 2000.

Ploetzner, R., Fehse, E., Kneser, C., and Spada, H. "Learning to Relate Qualitative and Quantitative Problem Representations in a Model-Based Setting for Collaborative Problem Solving." *Journal of the Learning Sciences,* 1999, *8*(2), 177–214.

Pokorny, R. A., Hall, E. P., Gallaway, M. A., and Dibble, E. "Analyzing Components of Work Samples to Evaluate Performance." *Military Psychology,* 1996, *8*(3), 161–177.

Polich, J. M., and Schwartz, S. H. "The Effect of Problem Size on Representation in Deductive Problem Solving." *Memory and Cognition,* 1974, *2*(4), 683–686.

Polkinghorne, D. *Narrative Knowing and the Human Sciences.* Albany: State University of New York Press, 1988.

Poole, M. S., and Holmes, M. E. "Decision Development in Computer-Assisted Group Decision Making." *Human Communication Research,* 1995, *22*(1), 90–127.

Popper, K. R. *All Life Is Problem Solving* (P. Carmiller, trans.). London: Routledge, 1999.

Postman, N. *The End of Education: Redefining the Value of School.* New York: Vintage, 1995.

Ranney, M., and Schank, P. "Modeling, Observing, and Promoting the Explanatory Coherence of Social Reasoning." In S. Read and L. Miller (eds.), *Connectionist and PDP Models of Social Reasoning.* Mahwah, N.J.: Erlbaum, 1998.

Read, S. J. "Constructing Causal Scenarios: A Knowledge Structure Approach to Causal Reasoning." *Journal of Personality and Social Psychology,* 1987, *52*(2), 288–302.

Reed, S. K., Willis, D., and Guarino, J. "Selecting Examples from Solving Word Problems." *Journal of Educational Psychology,* 1994, *86,* 380–388.

Renkl, A., Stark, R., Gruber, H., and Mandl, H. "Learning from Worked-Out Examples: The Effects of Example Variability and Elicited Self-Explanations." *Contemporary Educational Psychology,* 1998, *23,* 90–108.

Reusser, K. "Tutoring Systems and Pedagogical Theory: Representational Tools for Understanding, Planning, and Reflection in Problem Solving." In S. P. Lajoie and S. J. Derry (eds.), *Computers as Cognitive Tools.* Mahwah, N.J.: Erlbaum, 1993.

Riley, M. S., and Greeno, J. G. "Developmental Analysis of Understanding Language About Quantities in Solving Problems." *Cognition and Instruction,* 1988, *5*(1), 49–101.

Robertson, W. C. "Detection of Cognitive Structure with Protocol Data: Predicting Performance on Physics Transfer Problems." *Cognitive Science,* 1990, *14,* 253–280.

Savelsbergh, E. R., de Jong, T. and Ferguson-Hessler, M.G.M. "Competence-Related Differences in Problem Representations." In M. van Someren, P. Reimann, T. de Jong and H. Boshuizen (eds.), *The Role of Multiple Representations in Learning and Problem Solving* (pp. 262–282). Amsterdam: Elsevier Science, 1998.

Sanders, J. A., Wiseman, R. L., and Gass, R. H. "Does Teaching Argumentation Facilitate Critical Thinking?" *Communication Reports,* 1994, *7*(1), 27–35.

Schank, P., and Raney, M. "Assessing Explanatory Coherence: A New Method for Integrating Verbal Data with Models of On-Line Belief Revision." *Proceedings of the Fourteenth Annual Conference of the Cognitive Science Society.* Mahwah, N.J.: Erlbaum, 1992.

Schank, R. C. *Tell Me a Story: Narrative and Intelligence.* Evanston, Ill.: Northwestern University Press, 1990.

Schank, R. C. *Dynamic Memory Revisited.* Cambridge: Cambridge University Press, 1999.

Schank, R. C., and Abelson, R. *Scripts, Plans, Goals, and Understanding: An Inquiry into Human Knowledge Structures.* Mahwah, N.J.: Erlbaum, 1977.

Schank, R. C., Fano, A., Bell, B., and Jona, M. "The Design of Goal-Based Scenarios." *Journal of the Learning Sciences,* 1993/94, *3*(4), 305–346.

Schön, D. A. "Generative Metaphor: A Perspective on Problem-Setting in Social Policy." In A. Ortony (ed.), *Metaphor and Thought.* Cambridge: Cambridge University Press, 1979.

Schön, D. A. *The Reflective Practitioner—How Professionals Think in Action.* New York: Basic Books, 1993.

Schwartz, S. H. "Modes of Representation and Problem Solving: Well Evolved Is Half Solved." *Journal of Experimental Psychology,* 1971, *91,* 347–350.

Schwartz, S. H., and Fattaleh, D. L. "Representation in Deductive Problem Solving: The Matrix." *Journal of Experimental Psychology,* 1973, *95,* 343–348.

Sherrill, J. M. "Solving Textbook Mathematical Problems." *Alberta Journal of Educational Research,* 1983, *29,* 140–152.

Silver, E. A. "Recall of Mathematical Problem Information: Solving Related Problems." *Journal of Research in Mathematics Education,* 1981, *12,* 54–64.

Simon, D. P. "Information Processing Theory of Human Problem Solving." In D. Estes (ed.), *Handbook of Learning and Cognitive Process.* Mahwah, N.J.: Erlbaum, 1978.

Simon, H. A. "Studying Human Intelligence by Creating Artificial Intelligence." *American Scientist,* 1981, *69*(3), 300–309.

Sinnott, J. D. "A Model for Solution of Ill-Structured Problems: Implications for Everyday and Abstract Problem Solving." In J. D. Sinnott (ed.), *Everyday Problem Solving: Theory and Applications.* Westport, Conn.: Praeger, 1989.

Smith, M. U. "A View from Biology." In M. U. Smith (ed.), *Toward a Unified Theory of Problem Solving.* Mahwah, N.J.: Erlbaum, 1991.

Spiro, R. J., Coulson, R. L., Feltovich, P. J., and Anderson, D. K. *Cognitive Flexibility Theory: Advanced Knowledge Acquisition in Ill-Structured Domains.* Champaign: University of Illinois, Center for the Study of Reading, 1988.

Spiro, R. J., and Jehng, J. C. "Cognitive Flexibility and Hypertext: Theory and Technology for the Non-Linear and Multi-Dimensional Traversal of Complex Subject Matter." In D. Nix and R. J. Spiro (eds.), *Cognition, Education, and Multimedia: Explorations in High Technology.* Mahwah, N.J.: Erlbaum, 1990.

Spiro, R. J., and others. "Knowledge Acquisition for Application: Cognitive Flexibility and Transfer in Complex Content Domains." In B. C. Britton (ed.), *Executive Control Processes.* Mahwah, N.J.: Erlbaum, 1987.

Sternberg, R. J., and Frensch, P. A. (eds.). *Complex Problem Solving: Principles and Mechanisms.* Mahwah, N.J.: Erlbaum, 1991.

Suedfeld, P., de Vries, B., Bluck, S., and Wallbaum, B. C. "Intuitive Perceptions of Decision-Making Strategy: Naive Assessors' Concepts of Integrative Complexity." *International Journal of Psychology,* 1996, *31*(5), 177–190.

Sweller, J. "Cognitive Technology: Some Procedures for Facilitating Learning and Problem Solving in Mathematics and Science." *Journal of Educational Psychology,* 1989, *81*(4), 457–466.

Sweller, J., and Cooper, G. A. "The Use of Worked Examples as a Substitute for Problem Solving in Learning Algebra." *Cognition and Instruction,* 1985, *2*(1), 59–89.

Sweller, J., van Merrienboer, J.J.G., and Paas, F. G. "Cognitive Architecture and Instructional Design." *Educational Psychology Review,* 1998, *10* (3), 251–296.

Thagard, P. "Explaining Disease: Correlations, Causes, and Mechanisms." In F. C. Keil and R. A. Wilson (eds.), *Explanation and Cognition.* Cambridge, Mass.: MIT Press, 2000.

Toulmin, S. E. *The Uses of Argument.* Cambridge, England: University Press, 1958.

Toulmin, S. E., Rieke, R. D., and Janik, A. *An Introduction to Reasoning.* (2nd ed.) New York: Macmillan, 1984.

van der Veer, G. C. "Individual Differences and the User Interface." *Ergonomics,* 1989, *32*(11), 1431–1449.

Voss, J. F., Lawrence, J. A., and Engle, R. A. "From Representation to Decision: An Analysis of Problem Solving in International Relations." In R. J. Sternberg and P. A. French (eds.), *Complex Problem Solving.* Mahwah, N.J.: Erlbaum, 1991.

Voss, J. F., and Post, T. A. "On the Solving of Ill-Structured Problems." In M.T.H. Chi, R. Glaser, and M. J. Farr (eds.), *The Nature of Expertise.* Mahwah, N.J.: Erlbaum, 1988.

Voss, J. F., Wolfe, C. R., Lawrence, J. A., and Engle, J. A. "From Representation to Decision: An Analysis of Problem Solving in International Relations." In R. J. Sternberg and P. A. Frensch (eds.), *Complex Problem Solving: Principles and Mechanisms.* Mahwah, N.J.: Erlbaum, 1991.

Wagner, R. K. "Managerial Problem Solving." In R. J. Sternberg and P. A. Frensch (eds.), *Complex Problem Solving: Principles and Mechanisms.* Mahwah, N.J.: Erlbaum, 1991.

Wang, F. K., Jonassen, D. H., Strobel, J., and Cernusca, D. "Applications of a Case Library of Technology Integration Stories for Teachers." *Journal of Technology and Teacher Education,* forthcoming.

Ward, M., and Sweller, J. "Structuring Effective Worked Examples." *Cognition and Instruction,* 1990, *7*(1), 1–39.

Whimbey, A., and Lochhead, J. *Problem Solving and Comprehension.* (6th ed.) Mahwah, N.J.: Erlbaum, 1999.

White, B. "ThinkerTools: Causal Models, Conceptual Change, and Science Education." *Cognition and Instruction,* 1993, *10*(1), 1–100.

Williams, S. "Putting Case-Based Instruction into Context: Examples for Legal and Medical Education." *Journal of the Learning Sciences,* 1992, *2*(4), 367–427.

Wood, P. K. "Inquiring Systems and Problem Structures: Implications for Cognitive Development." *Human Development,* 1983, *26,* 249–265.

Yeh, S. S. "Empowering Education: Teaching Argumentative Writing to Cultural Minority Middle-School Students." *Research in the Teaching of English,* 1998, *33*(1), 49–83.

Young, M. F., Barab, S., and Garrett, S. "Agent as Detector: An Ecological Psychology Perspective on Learning by Perceiving-Acting Systems." In D. H. Jonassen and S. M. Land (eds.), *Theoretical Foundations of Learning Environments.* Mahwah, N.J.: Erlbaum, 2000.

Zhang, J. "The Nature of External Representation in Problem Solving." *Cognitive Science,* 1997, *21,* 179–217.

INDEX

A

Abelson, R., 64, 65

Absolute knowing, 36

Abstracted replays, 140–141

Abstractness of problems, 6

Actions, 136

Activity theory, 136

"Adventures of Jasper Woodbury" (video-based problems), 50

Aggregate planning environment case instruction, 54–55*fig*

Agogino, A. M., 68

Alessi, S., 121

Ambruso, D. J., 66, 106

Analogies, 166

Anchored instruction, 50–52

Anderson, D. K., 102

Anderson, J.R., 6, 59

ANIMATE, 29

ANOVA (analysis of variance) model of attribution, 64–65

Anzai, Y., 25

Arab-Israeli conflict systems model, 81*fig*

Argument construction, 123

Argumentation: assessing, 173–181*e*; described, 122–123; as problem representation tool, 44–45; skills used in, 123–124; technologies used in, 124–132. *See also* Justification

Argumentation assessment: coding student arguments for, 175–176; objective forms of, 173–174; of student essays/problem solving accounts, 176–181*e*

Argumentation technologies: Belvedere, 124–125, 129–130; Convince Me, 130–132; CSCA software, 124–125, 129–132; discussion forum, 125*fig*–129*fig*; scaffolded argumentation environment, 125–128, 175–176; SenseMaker, 128–129*fig*

The Art of Problem Posing (Brown and Walter), 48

David Jonassen is Distinguished Professor of Education at the University of Missouri, where he teaches in the areas of learning technologies and educational psychology. Since earning his doctorate in educational media and experimental educational psychology from Temple University, he has taught at the Pennsylvania State University, the University of Colorado, the University of Twente in the Netherlands, the University of North Carolina at Greensboro, and Syracuse University. He has published twenty-three books and numerous articles, papers, and reports on text design, task analysis, instructional design, computer-based learning, hypermedia, constructivist learning, cognitive tools, and technology in learning. He has consulted with businesses, universities, public schools, and other institutions around the world. His current research focuses on constructing design models and environments for problem solving.

Rita C. Richey is professor and program coordinator of instructional technology at Wayne State University. She has been at Wayne State for over thirty years and is experienced in not only program development, but also in education and training research. She has published widely in the areas of instructional design theory, including such books as *The Theoretical and Conceptual Bases of Instructional Design, Designing Instruction for the Adult Learner,* and *The Legacy of Robert M. Gagne.* Rita is coauthor of the third edition of *Instructional Design Competencies: The Standards* and the third edition of *Training Manager Competencies: The Standards.* She is also coauthor of *Instructional Technology: The Definition and Domains of the Field,* a book that received the 1995 Outstanding Book Award and the 1996 Brown Publication Award, both from the Association of Educational Communications and Technology. She has also received four major awards from Wayne State University: the President's Award for Excellence in Teaching, the Outstanding Graduate Mentor's Award, a Distinguished Faculty Fellowship, and an award for Outstanding Scholarly Achievement by Women Faculty. In addition, she has been elected to the Wayne State University Academy of Scholars. In recognition of her career's work, she received the AECT Distinguished Service Award in 2000.

William J. Rothwell, Ph.D., SPHR certification, is professor in charge of the workforce education and development program in the Department of Learning and Performance Systems at Pennsylvania State University. He is also president of Rothwell and Associates, Inc., an independent consulting firm. He has been a training director in a government agency and a large insurance company, a consultant to many organizations, and a college professor.

William is the author and coauthor of many books. His most recent publications include *Mastering the Instructional Design Process: A Systematic Approach,* 3rd edition (with H.C. Kazanas, 2004), *The Strategic Development of Talent* (with H.C. Kazanas, 2003), *What CEOs Expect from Corporate Training: Building Workplace Learning and Performance Initiatives That Advance Organizational Goals* (with J. Lindholm and W. Wallick, 2003), *Planning and Managing Human Resources,* 2nd edition (with H.C. Kazanas, 2003), *Creating Sales Training and Development Programs: A Competency-Based Approach to Building Sales Ability* (with W. Donahue and J. Park, 2002), *The Workplace Learner: How to Align Training Initiatives with Individual Learning Competencies* (2002), and *Building Effective Technical Training: How to Develop Hard Skills Within Organizations* (with J. Benkowski, 2002).

In his consulting work, William specializes in human resources practices—particularly in competency modeling and succession planning and management.

Timothy W. Spannaus, Ph.D., is senior lecturer in instructional technology and research fellow with the Institute for Learning and Performance Improvement, at Wayne State University. He is also chief learning architect at The Emdicium Group, Inc., in Southfield, Michigan.

Tim is president of the International Board of Standards for Training, Performance, and Instruction and was previously president of the Association for Development of Computer-Based Instructional Systems. He is active in the International Society for Performance Improvement and the American Society for Training and Development.

His teaching, research, and development focus on interactive technologies for learning and performance improvement. Recent projects include the creation of a training vision for a major municipal utility, the design and development of web-based learning courses, and a knowledge management plan for a Fortune 500 manufacturer. Recent publications include *Training Manager Competencies: The Standards*, two chapters in the *ID Casebook*—a forthcoming book on development of web-based learning—and numerous papers and presentations.

**Kent L. Gustafson,** Ph.D., is professor emeritus of instructional technology at the University of Georgia, where he was chair of the department and taught courses in instructional design, research, and management of technology-based education programs. He has published three books and numerous articles, book chapters, and technical reports. Kent is a regular presenter at major educational conferences in the United States and has spoken in many other countries including Australia, Iran, Japan, Korea, the Netherlands, Malaysia, Mexico, Nicaragua, the Philippines, and Switzerland. He is also former president of the Association for Educational Communications and Technology. Kent's research interest includes design and evaluation of electronic performance support systems, management of technology design and delivery, and professional education of technologists.

M. David Merrill, Ph.D., is professor in the department of instructional technology at Utah State University. He is also the owner and president of Ascape, Tennsion & Sulphur Gulch RR. Recognized as a leader in instructional design,

David is listed among the most productive educational psychologists (*Educational Researcher,* 1984), the most frequently cited authors in the computer-based instruction literature (*Journal of Computer-Based Instruction,* 1987), and the most influential people in the field of instructional technology (*Performance & Instruction,* 1988.) As a major contributor in his field, David was the recipient of the Association for Educational Communications and Technology's 2001 Distinguished Service Award for advancing the field of instructional technology through scholarship, teaching, and leadership. His current work involves the identification of First Principles of Instruction.

Allison Rossett, Ed.D., is professor of educational technology at San Diego State University, with academic focus on workforce development, e-learning, and needs assessment. Allison received the American Society for Training and Development's award for Workplace Learning and Performance for 2002 and will join its International Board in January 2004. She is also a member of *Training* magazine's HRD Hall of Fame, the editor of the *ASTD E-Learning Handbook: Best Practices, Strategies, and Case Studies for an Emerging Field,* and co-author of *Beyond the Podium: Delivering Training and Performance to a Digital World.* Allison has worked with a who's who of international organizations, including IBM, Microsoft, MetLife, the Internal Revenue Service, Hewlett-Packard, SQL Star International, Ford Motor Company, SBC, and Fidelity Investments.

Pfeiffer Publications Guide

This guide is designed to familiarize you with the various types of Pfeiffer publications. The formats section describes the various types of products that we publish; the methodologies section describes the many different ways that content might be provided within a product. We also provide a list of the topic areas in which we publish.

FORMATS

In addition to its extensive book-publishing program, Pfeiffer offers content in an array of formats, from fieldbooks for the practitioner to complete, ready-to-use training packages that support group learning.

FIELDBOOK Designed to provide information and guidance to practitioners in the midst of action. Most fieldbooks are companions to another, sometimes earlier, work, from which its ideas are derived; the fieldbook makes practical what was theoretical in the original text. Fieldbooks can certainly be read from cover to cover. More likely, though, you'll find yourself bouncing around following a particular theme, or dipping in as the mood, and the situation, dictate.

HANDBOOK A contributed volume of work on a single topic, comprising an eclectic mix of ideas, case studies, and best practices sourced by practitioners and experts in the field.

An editor or team of editors usually is appointed to seek out contributors and to evaluate content for relevance to the topic. Think of a handbook not as a ready-to-eat meal, but as a cookbook of ingredients that enables you to create the most fitting experience for the occasion.

RESOURCE Materials designed to support group learning. They come in many forms: a complete, ready-to-use exercise (such as a game); a comprehensive resource on one topic (such as conflict management) containing a variety of methods and approaches; or a collection of like-minded activities (such as icebreakers) on multiple subjects and situations.

TRAINING PACKAGE An entire, ready-to-use learning program that focuses on a particular topic or skill. All packages comprise a guide for the facilitator/trainer and a workbook for the participants. Some packages are supported with additional media—such as video—or learning aids, instruments, or other devices to help participants understand concepts or practice and develop skills.

- *Facilitator/trainer's guide* Contains an introduction to the program, advice on how to organize and facilitate the learning event, and step-by-step instructor notes. The guide also contains copies of presentation materials—handouts, presentations, and overhead designs, for example—used in the program.

- *Participant's workbook* Contains exercises and reading materials that support the learning goal and serves as a valuable reference and support guide for participants in the weeks and months that follow the learning event. Typically, each participant will require his or her own workbook.

ELECTRONIC CD-ROMs and Web-based products transform static Pfeiffer content into dynamic, interactive experiences. Designed to take advantage of the searchability, automation, and ease-of-use that technology provides, our e-products bring convenience and immediate accessibility to your workspace.

METHODOLOGIES

CASE STUDY A presentation, in narrative form, of an actual event that has occurred inside an organization. Case studies are not prescriptive, nor are they used to prove a point; they are designed to develop critical analysis and decision-making skills. A case study has a specific time frame, specifies a sequence of events, is narrative in structure, and contains a plot structure—an issue (what should be/have been done?). Use case studies when the goal is to enable participants to apply previously learned theories to the circumstances in the case, decide what is pertinent, identify the real issues, decide what should have been done, and develop a plan of action.

ENERGIZER A short activity that develops readiness for the next session or learning event. Energizers are most commonly used after a break or lunch to stimulate or refocus the group. Many involve some form of physical activity, so they are a useful way to counter post-lunch lethargy. Other uses include transitioning from one topic to another, where "mental" distancing is important.

EXPERIENTIAL LEARNING ACTIVITY (ELA) A facilitator-led intervention that moves participants through the learning cycle from experience to application (also known as a Structured Experience). ELAs are carefully thought-out designs in which there is a definite learning purpose and intended outcome. Each step—everything that participants do during the activity—facilitates the accomplishment of the stated goal. Each ELA includes complete instructions for facilitating the intervention and a clear statement of goals, suggested group size and timing, materials required, an explanation of the process, and, where appropriate, possible variations to the activity. (For more detail on Experiential Learning Activities, see the Introduction to the *Reference Guide to Handbooks and Annuals*, 1999 edition, Pfeiffer, San Francisco.)

GAME A group activity that has the purpose of fostering team spirit and togetherness in addition to the achievement of a pre-stated goal. Usually contrived—undertaking a desert expedition, for example—this type of learning method offers an engaging means for participants to demonstrate and practice business and interpersonal skills. Games are effective for team building and personal development mainly because the goal is subordinate to the process—the means through which participants reach decisions, collaborate, communicate, and generate trust and understanding. Games often engage teams in "friendly" competition.

ICEBREAKER A (usually) short activity designed to help participants overcome initial anxiety in a training session and/or to acquaint the participants with one another. An icebreaker can be a fun activity or can be tied to specific topics or training goals. While a useful tool in itself, the icebreaker comes into its own in situations where tension or resistance exists within a group.

INSTRUMENT A device used to assess, appraise, evaluate, describe, classify, and summarize various aspects of human behavior. The term used to describe an instrument depends primarily on its format and purpose. These terms include survey, questionnaire, inventory, diagnostic, survey, and poll. Some uses of instruments include providing instrumental feedback to group members, studying here-and-now processes or functioning within a group, manipulating group composition, and evaluating outcomes of training and other interventions.

Instruments are popular in the training and HR field because, in general, more growth can occur if an individual is provided with a method for focusing specifically on his or her own behavior. Instruments also are used to obtain information that will serve as a basis for change and to assist in workforce planning efforts.

Paper-and-pencil tests still dominate the instrument landscape with a typical package comprising a facilitator's guide, which offers advice on administering the instrument and interpreting the collected data, and an initial set of instruments. Additional instruments are available separately. Pfeiffer, though, is investing heavily in e-instruments. Electronic instrumentation provides effortless distribution and, for larger groups particularly, offers advantages over paper-and-pencil tests in the time it takes to analyze data and provide feedback.

LECTURETTE A short talk that provides an explanation of a principle, model, or process that is pertinent to the participants' current learning needs. A lecturette is intended to establish a common language bond between the trainer and the participants by providing a mutual frame of reference. Use a lecturette as an introduction to a group activity or event, as an interjection during an event, or as a handout.

MODEL A graphic depiction of a system or process and the relationship among its elements. Models provide a frame of reference and something more tangible, and more easily remembered, than a verbal explanation. They also give participants something to "go on," enabling them to track their own progress as they experience the dynamics, processes, and relationships being depicted in the model.

ROLE PLAY A technique in which people assume a role in a situation/scenario: a customer service rep in an angry-customer exchange, for example. The way in which the role is approached is then discussed and feedback is offered. The role play is often repeated using a different approach and/or incorporating changes made based on feedback received. In other words, role playing is a spontaneous interaction involving realistic behavior under artificial (and safe) conditions.

SIMULATION A methodology for understanding the interrelationships among components of a system or process. Simulations differ from games in that they test or use a model that depicts or mirrors some aspect of reality in form, if not necessarily in content. Learning occurs by studying the effects of change on one or more factors of the model. Simulations are commonly used to test hypotheses about what happens in a system—often referred to as "what if?" analysis—or to examine best-case/worst-case scenarios.

THEORY A presentation of an idea from a conjectural perspective. Theories are useful because they encourage us to examine behavior and phenomena through a different lens.

TOPICS

The twin goals of providing effective and practical solutions for workforce training and organization development and meeting the educational needs of training and human resource professionals shape Pfeiffer's publishing program. Core topics include the following:

Leadership & Management

Communication & Presentation

Coaching & Mentoring

Training & Development

E-Learning

Teams & Collaboration

OD & Strategic Planning

Human Resources

Consulting

What will you find on pfeiffer.com?

- The best in workplace performance solutions for training and HR professionals

- Downloadable training tools, exercises, and content

- Web-exclusive offers

- Training tips, articles, and news

- Seamless on-line ordering

- Author guidelines, information on becoming a Pfeiffer Affiliate, and much more

Discover more at www.pfeiffer.com

Customer Care

Have a question, comment, or suggestion? Contact us! We value your feedback and we want to hear from you.

For questions about this or other Pfeiffer products, you may contact us by:

E-mail: **customer@wiley.com**

Mail: **Customer Care Wiley/Pfeiffer**
10475 Crosspoint Blvd.
Indianapolis, IN 46256

Phone: **(US) 800-274-4434** (Outside the US: 317-572-3985)

Fax: **(US) 800-569-0443** (Outside the US: 317-572-4002)

To order additional copies of this title or to browse other Pfeiffer products, visit us online at **www.pfeiffer.com**.

For **Technical Support** questions, call **(800) 274-4434.**

For authors guidelines, log on to www.pfeiffer.com and click on "Resources for Authors."

If you are . . .

A **college bookstore, a professor, an instructor, or work in higher education** and you'd like to place an order or request an exam copy, please contact jbreview@wiley.com.

A **general retail bookseller** and you'd like to establish an account or speak to a local sales representative, contact Melissa Grecco at 201-748-6267 or mgrecco@wiley.com.

An **exclusively on-line bookseller**, contact Amy Blanchard at 530-756-9456 or ablanchard @wiley.com or Jennifer Johnson at 206-568-3883 or jjohnson@wiley.com, both of our Online Sales department.

A **librarian or library representative**, contact John Chambers in our Library Sales department at 201-748-6291 or jchamber@wiley.com.

A **reseller, training company/consultant, or corporate trainer**, contact Charles Regan in our Special Sales department at 201-748-6553 or cregan@wiley.com.

A **specialty retail distributor** (includes specialty gift stores, museum shops, and corporate bulk sales), contact Kim Hendrickson in our Special Sales department at 201-748-6037 or khendric@wiley.com.

Purchasing for the **Federal government**, contact Ron Cunningham in our Special Sales department at 317-572-3053 or rcunning@wiley.com.

Purchasing for a **State or Local government**, contact Charles Regan in our Special Sales department at 201-748-6553 or cregan@wiley.com.